QUICKBOOKS

The Complete Guide to Master Bookkeeping and Accounting for Small Businesses

DWIGHT ROACH

© **Copyright 2019 by Dwight Roach**
All rights reserved.

This document is geared towards providing exact and reliable information with regards to the topic and issue covered. The publication is sold with the idea that the publisher is not required to render accounting, officially permitted, or otherwise qualified services. If advice is necessary, legal or professional, a practiced individual in the profession should be ordered.

- From a Declaration of Principles which was accepted and approved equally by a Committee of the American Bar Association and a Committee of Publishers and Associations.

In no way is it legal to reproduce, duplicate, or transmit any part of this document in either electronic means or in printed format. Recording of this publication is strictly prohibited, and any storage of this document is not allowed unless with written permission from the publisher. All rights reserved.

The information provided herein is stated to be truthful and consistent, in that any liability, in terms of inattention or otherwise, by any usage or abuse of any policies, processes, or directions contained within is the solitary and utter responsibility of the recipient reader. Under no circumstances will any legal responsibility or blame be held against the publisher for any reparation, damages, or monetary loss due to the information herein, either directly or indirectly.

Respective authors own all copyrights not held by the publisher.

The information herein is offered for informational purposes solely and is universal as so. The presentation of the information is without a contract or any type of guarantee assurance.

The trademarks that are used are without any consent, and the publication of the trademark is without permission or backing by the trademark owner. All trademarks and brands within this book are for clarifying purposes only and are owned by the owners themselves, not affiliated with this document.

TABLE OF CONTENTS

Introduction 1

Chapter 1: Getting Started 4

What Is Quickbooks 4

Why Is It Important For Small And Large Business To Use Quickbooks 4

How Can Your Business Benefit From Quickbooks? ... 9

Information To Help You Get Started 10

Navigating The Workplace 11

How Your Accounting Methods Affect Quickbooks .. 16

Chapter 2: Quick Manual Configuration 19

Entering Tax Information 26

Tracking Sales Orders 27

Completing The Company Configuration Process 33

Computation Of Excess Payment 38

Chapter 3: How Can I Enter Customer And Vendor 47

Build Your Client List 47

Sales Tax Settings 50

Payment Options For Customers 52

Personalize Client List And Features 55

Use Features 58

Active And Inactive Customers 61

Tax Settings 69

Chapter 4: Entry And Payment Of Bills 80

Account Processing In Quickbooks 80

Paying Bills With Quickbooks 80
How Quickbooks Records Payments To Your Account
.... 85
Apply Vendor Discounts To Account Payments 86

Chapter 5: Bank Account And Records 89

How To Write A Cheque 89
Common Features Of Quickbooks Records 91
Entering A Cheque Manually 92
Transfer Between Accounts 94
Reconciliation Of Bank Account 95

Chapter 6: Payroll 98

Set Time Tracking 98
Use Of Weekly Schedule 104
Change Entries In A Report 107
Mileage Tracking 111
Quickbooks Desktop Payroll Services 115
Custom Setup For Payroll 123

Chapter 7: Pay Employees, Pay Taxes, And Creating
Forms 129

Handle Year Payment Data 129
Company Preparation Department 133
Manage Your Salary 137
Allocation Of Staff Center 141
Check For Faults 148
State And Local Income Tax 152

INTRODUCTION

QuickBooks is an accounting software solution for small business owners. It tracks income and expenses, prepares billings and payroll, organizes customers' information, and more. But like any piece of software, it requires learning the jargon and the steps to become proficient, as it can effectively manage all your accounting needs.

Although most small business owners take care of their business, but it involves many other responsibilities. You will need to invoice the customer, pay a registration fee to the customer, pay your bill to the vendor, manage inventory, and - in your "free time" - analyze financial data to see the next focused effort. QuickBooks is a tool that you can use to automate tasks already done by business owners. When you use QuickBooks, you spend most of your time on forms, lists, or records.

MAKING USE OF FORM

You record most of your business transactions on a daily basis. The QuickBooks form looks like a paper form. The form is simple - you already know how to fill out a form. However, when you provide information in the form of QuickBooks, it will do the accounting for you in the background. For example, when you sign up for an invoice and then write a cheque (sold through payment accounts) to pay for the business, QuickBooks merges the transaction into its liabilities.

Prove the costs and payments you generate. (Accounts due "Accounts Payable" is money owed to the vendor.) It also records the cheque in your bank account, updates the records, and provides a current balance of the amount you owe.

MAKING USE OF LIST

This list is another essential feature of QuickBooks. Most QuickBooks forms can be completed by selecting items from the list.

QuickBooks has a list where you can store information about customers, suppliers, employees, goods or services for sale, and more. The listings save time and help you put the information together all the time. When you fill out an invoice form and select a customer name from the "Customer: Business" list, QuickBooks not only fills in the name but also completes the customer's address, payment terms, and sales tax.

QuickBooks lets you use the menu buttons at the bottom of each list to complete various list activities. For example, to fill a customer account, first, select a customer from the Customer Work list, and then select Create Account from the Activities menu.

MAKING USE OF RECORD

In addition to forms and lists, you will also use records from QuickBooks. Just like you use cheque entry registration to view the records of all transactions in your bank account

In writing, other payments you have in your account and deposits - QuickBooks records contain records of all activities in your account. Almost every QuickBooks account has its own record.

CHAPTER 1: GETTING STARTED

What is QuickBooks

QuickBooks is a small business accounting software that helps companies manage revenue and expenses and keep track of day-to-day transactions. You can use it for invoicing customers, paying bills, generating plan reports, tax returns, and more. The QuickBooks product line includes several solutions for everyone, from entrepreneurs to mid-sized companies.

Since there are a number of QuickBooks software, it is essential to choose the right one. To choose the right one, please register for a 30-day free trial. This trial is a fully-featured version of QuickBooks. This way, you can test all the ringtones. The most interesting aspect of it is that no credit card is required.

Why Is It Important For Small and Large Business to Use Quickbooks

SME owners normally use QuickBooks to manage their accounts, pay their bills, and track their cash flow. They also use it to produce monthly and annual reports, as well as to prepare quarterly or annual income taxes. Business owners typically run QuickBooks themselves or use internal or external accountants.

The following are a few benefits of QuickBooks:

1. To manage sales and revenue

You can manage sales and revenue on QuickBooks by creating a sales tracking account for your customers. Keep track of the amount owed to you by your customers (also known as accounts receivable) by reviewing the due date report, which details current and expired invoices.

2. Keep track of bills and fees

By linking your bank account and credit card to QuickBooks, QuickBooks automatically tracks your bills and expenses, so you can take on all expenses and categorize them. If you need to keep track of cheques or cash transactions, you can record them directly on QuickBooks in minutes.

QuickBooks can also help you pay your bills when they expire. For example, you can ensure timely payments by creating a vendor report in less than two minutes. Get detailed information on current and expired invoices in this report to make sure you get started quickly.

3. Learn about your business

By managing all the cash flow and cash outflow activities on QuickBooks, you can access multiple reports that provide valuable insight into your business.

All reports are prepared in QuickBooks and can be done with just a few clicks. When you enter and save a transaction, the report is updated in real-time.

It would be useful if you need to provide funds to potential investors or lenders for small business credit lines. In addition to the debtor reports and payability reports we discussed earlier, you can also create the first three reports that are required to evaluate the overall health of your business:

- ✓ Profit and loss statement
- ✓ Balance sheet report
- ✓ Cash flow statement

Profit and loss statement

Profit and loss statements can be created in minutes. By summing up revenue minus expenses, you can show your profitability. It shows your net profit (loss) over a period of time (for example, a week, a month, or a quarter). The following is a statement of profit and loss for the fictional entity, Paul's Water Supply, from January 1 to September 29, 2016:

Balance sheet report

The balance sheet is a statement of the company's assets and liabilities for a given day called the balance sheet date (e.g., at the end of a given financial year). Assets presented in the balance sheet are resources controlled by the company. On the other hand, liabilities show all sources of financing for these resources. Create a Balance Sheet Report in QuickBooks with just a few clicks.

Cash flow statement

At QuickBooks, you can quickly create a cash flow statement. The report shows you all the activities that affect business cash inflows and outflows.

4. Perform payroll calculation

Salary is an area you do not want to do manually. Errors in the computation of salaries can lead to high fines and unhappy employees. To solve this problem, QuickBooks has its own billing feature that automatically calculates and manages billing based on your needs.

The interesting thing about using QuickBooks payroll is that it's built into QuickBooks, so your financial statements are always updated after you last started your invoice. You need to purchase a QuickBooks billing subscription to access the latest billing tables to calculate employee and employer pay.

QuickBooks can help you do the following:

- ✓ Pay employees by cheque or direct deposit
- ✓ Federal and state-level payroll taxes are automatically calculated

- ✓ QuickBooks will fill out a payroll tax form.
- ✓ You can pay directly from QuickBooks through online payment.

5. Inventory tracking

If you need to track inventory for sale, for example, QuickBooks automatically tracks and updates the amount available and the unit price when entering a transaction. QuickBooks provides some inventory management reports. Although inventory tracking in an Excel spreadsheet is possible, it can be time-consuming.

6. Simplify taxation

If you still don't believe you can use QuickBooks to simplify your taxes, consider your fear of the tax season. Whether you need to consolidate multiple Excel spreadsheets or organize a shoebox full of receipts, it will take longer for tax professionals to get what they need compared to preparing your tax return!

7. Accept online payment

One of the easiest ways to enhance cash flow is to allow customers to pay their bills online. With QuickBooks, you can add Intuit Payments at the touch of a button.

Once activated, any invoices that you email will include a "pay now" button. Your client can click on this button and make a payment using one of their major credit cards or authorize ACH payment directly from their bank account by entering their bank account information.

How Can Your Business Benefit From Quickbooks?

Money management

QuickBooks has the ability to help small businesses manage their money. The program aspect allows the user to enter an expiration date and payment information for all duplicate accounts. As the invoice expires, users can print the cheque directly from QuickBooks. In addition, each transaction is recorded for easier access in future reviews. QuickBooks users can also link their bank account to the program. This feature not only allows you to view all your financial records on a single screen but also the advantage of not requiring paper reports.

Cost report

When doing business, professionals typically pay different fees before billing a consumer. These can be small purchases, such as mileage and meals, or large fees, such as longer international travel. No matter what the size or type of spending, QuickBooks has a feature that allows users to record their personal expenses. Additionally, depending on the customer or business, cost savings can be achieved so that the user does not have to adjust costs manually.

Sales order

QuickBooks offers time-saving sales tracking and automatic receipt and invoice creation with the push of a button. The invoice can then be sent electronically to the buyer via email. Through the program, customers can also pay bills separately or in bulk. This last feature is especially useful when charging more customers for the same service. An added benefit for customers who subscribe to Intuit QuickBooks Merchant Services is the ability to accept credit and debit card fees through QuickBooks. In addition, users who subscribe to QuickBooks' Intuit Cheque Solution can scan the cheque and place it in the program, so there is no need to enter information manually.

The report

Users of QuickBooks Pro can create various financial statements. These include annual revenue, expenditures, trends, and forecast documentation. Also, any report can be exported to Ms. Excel worksheet format and sent electronically via email.

Easy to use

The maker of QuickBooks Pro made the software easy to use. The new user configuration feature allows users to create virtual orientations. In addition, most program features can be activated at the touch of a button.

Information to help you get started

If you are not familiar with QuickBooks, a startup window will pop up when you open a company file. This window will guide you through the steps to complete after installation. Company Profile To display the Getting Started window, select Start from the Help menu.

If you are upgrading from an older version, QuickBooks will display a new feature. This window provides information about new functions and shows you how to find what you need to get started with the latest version. To view the new feature window, select New features from the Help menu.

Navigating the Workplace

There are numerous ways to get what you need in the QuickBooks workspace.

Start the browser

The QuickBooks viewer provides a graphical representation of the workflow for a specific product area. For example, the Buyer browser window contains icons for important activities that are shared with clients and sold (for example, creating invoices, receiving payments, and making deposit payments).

The browser gives you access to the features, reports, and solutions of the main areas of QuickBooks.

- The organizational chart guides you through the tasks in the correct order.
- Related activities and stored reports will allow you to analyze data and take action.
- Client solutions help you find features and services you can use to run your business.

To view a browser, select its name from the list of browsers.

To get more workspace on your current assignment, QuickBooks normally display one window at a time. If you open a new window, it will show in front of the previously opened window.

A list of open windows tracks open windows. While working, use a list of open windows to switch between windows. If you want to switch to another open window, just click on the title of the window you want to display.

Show or hide the open window:

- From the View menu, select Open Window List.

If the list is currently displayed, a match will appear on the left side of the menu item.

In comparison, you may want to display multiple windows at once. You can easily switch between one window and multiple windows at a time. When you select multiple windows from the show menu, QuickBooks adds a title to the window in the main part. You can then move the window and resize as needed.

To view multiple sales:

In the View menu, select More Windows.

Use the menu bar

You can find all the QuickBooks commands in the menu bar.

Some commands in the menu bar can be added to the icon bar.

All the accounts you need to know

QuickBooks does not require users to learn or understand accounting terms. However, it does use some common business conditions. Assets include the one own and the assets you owe. The person who owes you money is called accounts receivable, receivable, or receivable. QuickBooks uses receivables to track past-

13

due liabilities. The rest of the company's assets may include cheques, savings accounts, petty cash, fixed assets (such as equipment or cars), inventories, and "no deposit" (money you receive from clients but not yet deposited with the bank).

When you start a company in QuickBooks, keep in mind that bank accounts, savings, and pocket money are assets of the company, and you will install them as a "bank" account in QuickBooks.

Debt is the amount your company owes. The amount you owe on your unpaid account is payable invoices, "Payable Invoices," or short-term "Payable Invoices." QuickBooks uses accounts payable to track accounts you owe to others.

When setting up company files in QuickBooks, keep in mind that while unpaid invoices are "liabilities," you will install them as "Accounts Payable" in "Credibility" in QuickBooks.

The capital

Equity - "equity" - is the difference between the assets (assets) you own and the debts (debts):

Equity = assets - liabilities

If you sell all your assets today and use the money you sell to sell your debt to pay off debt, the rest of your money is your capital.

Your capital reflects the health of your business because it is the money you have left to repay all your debts. The funding source comes from the following three aspects:

- Owner investment in the company
- Net profit from operating activities during the accounting period
- Retained earnings not allocated to the owner or net income from the previous period

Of course, as an owner, you can also raise funds from your business. This withdrawal is called "owner withdrawal" and reduces commercial capital.

If you have unique assets (the existence of a business depends entirely on your efforts), you can cheque the equity value by creating a balance sheet on QuickBooks.

Cash and Accumulated Accounting

The money

Many small businesses get records of their income and expenses when they receive bills. This method is called cash accounting. If you make a deposit from a client and you do not owe money as part of your income, you should always use the cash system. Similarly, if you already registered a cat at the time of payment, you used a cash basis.

15

Cumulative cardinality

In cumulative accounting, you record revenue at the time of sale, not when you receive payment. Similarly, you enter a fee when you receive an invoice, not when you pay.

Most accountants believe that a cumulative approach can give you a more realistic financial position for your business.

How Your Accounting Methods Affect QuickBooks

If you use cash or the cumulative method, you can merge transactions in the same way at QuickBooks.

QuickBooks is set up, so you have to collect reports. For example, even if you did not receive an invoice, you will be assigned a profit and loss statement immediately after you register the invoice.

Payment. Once you register your invoice, file your invoice immediately, even if you haven't paid.

You can view any report (except the transaction report) in cash by changing your settings. (In the Edit menu, select Preferences. In the Preferences window, click Reports and Charts, and then click Preferred.)

Measuring business profit

The two most important reports that measure business profits are the balance sheet and income statement. These are the reports most commonly created by accountants and financial staff. (For example, when you apply for a loan, the bank will ask for two documents at a time.)

State status

A status report is a financial statement of your company on a specific date. It means:

- ✓ what you have (assets)
- ✓ what you are owed (receivables)
- ✓ Your company owes it to others (responsibility and debts)
- ✓ The net profit (equity) of your business

Example of status view

1. In the "Reports" menu, select "Company and Finance."
2. In the submenu, select "Standard Balance Sheet."

Profit and loss (also known as the income statement)

The income statement shows income, expenses, and net profit or loss (equal to revenue minus expenses).

To view the income statement:

1. In the "Reports" menu, select "Company and Finance."
2. In the submenu, select "Profit and Loss Standards."

Liquidity flow reporting

Another report that may interest you is the cash flow statement. The Liquidity Flow Report shows your income and expenses over a given accounting period.

To view the fluid flow report:

1. In the "Reports" menu, select "Company and Finance."
2. In the submenu, select "Cash Flow Statement."

Getting out of QuickBooks

Like most other Windows programs, QuickBooks does not require you to tax your information before leaving it. The amount of information stored depends on how much you use QuickBooks.

Quit QuickBooks:

- In the File menu, select Exit

Unless you open another application, QuickBooks will take you to your Windows desktop.

To prevent or reduce data loss, you should periodically back up your data from QuickBooks. If data loss occurs, you can restore it from a backup. Back up the File menu and select Backup.

CHAPTER 2: QUICK MANUAL CONFIGURATION

Create a company on QuickBooks

QuickBooks contains all the financial records for one job. Before using QuickBooks, you need to save your job to QuickBooks before you can install business files.

How many companies can you configure?

If you have a multi-company business, DGII wants you to clearly list all sources of revenue and record all business expenses you need to subtract. Therefore, for tax purposes, it is usually best to install a separate QuickBooks company for each commercial entity that you file on your tax form.

About "Easy Step Interview"

The Easy Step Interview will guide you through the process of setting up your business on QuickBooks. Interviews were analyzed in sections. You must first complete the general section. If you are having a problem answering the question, you can always go back and change your response later.

The "Easy Step Interview" is divided into five sections:

The General Section - Allows you to enter company information, select an account directory that is suitable for your business, specify QuickBooks settings, and set a start date for your business.

Revenue and Expense "Revenue and Expense" - allows you to view income and expense accounts for your account directory and merge new accounts.

Detailed Revenue Details - Allows you to determine if your business revenue comes from services and / or products being sold. On the basis of the information provided, QuickBooks will decide what portions of the income and accounts due will be used.

Opening Balance - Allows you to enter information about the buyer who owes on the start date and the seller you owe.

What next? This section presents some of the common tasks in QuickBooks. After completing the rest of the interview, you may want to complete these tasks.

Each part of the interview is divided into topics that appear at the top of the Easy Step Interview window. After completing a question or chapter, QuickBooks displays a checkmark on the card.

Review the interview

Click Next to display the following chat window.

Click "Previous" to display the previous interview window.

When the window has more buttons (bottom right), click to see more details about the questions asked in the interview. After reading the details, you will then click "OK" It will automatically take you back the interview page.

Click "Leave" to leave the interview and go back to QuickBooks. You can return to the interview at a later date by opening the company file and selecting "Easy Step Interview" from the "File" option. QuickBooks will remember the information you enter.

Initialize "Easy Step Interviews"

Initialize a new company:

1. Start QuickBooks
2. Select "Create a new company" or select "New company" from the "Quick Fix" menu "Files" in the "Easy Step Interview" window.

Entering your business information

When you create a new company in QuickBooks using Easy Step Interviews, QuickBooks asks you what type of business you have. Use your answers to get started quickly and set up the right accounts and lists. In this course, you will create a new company at QuickBooks for a company called Lockhart Design. Margaret Lockhart is the sole owner of this interior design company. Most of its revenue comes from consulting services, but it also sells products like fabrics and accessories to customers.

To create a new company file in QuickBooks:

1. In the first interview window, type "Next" to get started.
2. Keep typing "Next" and read the information in the Welcome window until the Welcome section is complete.

Upon completion of this section, QuickBooks will highlight the tabs.

3. Click Next (Next) until the "Company Name" screen appears on the "Company Information" tab.
4. In the Company name box, type "Block Design" and press the TAB key.

When you press the TAB key, QuickBooks automatically enters the name you entered in the Legal Name field. QuickBooks uses the company name in all reports.

23

5. Click "Next"
6. Enter the following information in the "Address of your company" window. 613 NW 2nd Ter, Deerfield Beach, FL, 33441.

QuickBooks prints this company's address on cheques, invoices, and other forms.

7. Click "Next"
8. In the "Other Company Information" tab, enter the following data:
   - Make sure you select "January" in the first month of the income tax year and the first month of the fiscal year. QuickBooks uses the fiscal year of your choice to create the latest report.
   - Set the default province to British Columbia
   - Set company number "company number" to 123456789. The screen should look like this.
9. Click "Next" to continue

Use the default account directory.

The account directory lists the accounts in the balance sheets, income, and expense accounts. When you create a new company in QuickBooks, you can choose the type of company that is as close as possible to your business type, and QuickBooks will install an account directory for you. It also installs other listings that match your types of business, such as payment method, customer and supplier type, and payment terms. The type of business you choose will affect the account directory QuickBooks installs for you. Even if you have a type of company that is not explicitly listed, choose the company closest to you, so get an advantage in creating your own account directory. After QuickBooks creates an account directory for you, you can modify it as needed.

Create an account directory:

1. In the "Select Business Unit" option, select "Retail: General" from the "Industry" list and click "Next."

Although Lockhart Design generates revenue from a consultant rather than a retailer, the type of retailer provides the maximum number of accounts we need. We will later need to modify the account directory to include a consultancy revenue account.

2. Double-click "Next" to open the "Save As" window.
3. Check that QuickBooks are ready to save files to the KB train folder4. In the file name "New Company" of the window, click "Save" to accept the name "Lockhart Design." QuickBooks creates company files and then displays a list of income and expenses available to retailers in this account directory.

4. Confirm that "Yes" is selected to familiarize you with these accounts, and then click "Next."
5. In the Visit Company window, keep the number of employees who will access QuickBooks as 0, and then click Next.
6. Press Next until you scroll from Company Information to Preferred.
7. A "No password" warning message will be displayed, click "No" to continue. You can set a password later as needed.

Adjust the settings in QuickBooks

In the Easy Step Interviews settings section, you can indicate whether you want to use some features of QuickBooks. From the interview you can choose:

- Number of stocks; whether or not it can be activated depending on whether your business maintains inventory.
- Sales tax
- The invoice format you want to use pay list
- Estimated Bid (QuickBooks Pro and Premier Only)
- Progress Invoice is Progress Invoice (QuickBooks Pro and Premier only)
- Purchase Orders "Sales Orders" (QuickBooks Pro and Premier, only)
- Time tracking "Time tracking" (QuickBooks Pro and Premier only)

- Classes
- How do you want to record the invoices: directly on the cheque or by entering the invoices and then the payment
- Remainders reminders

Entering tax information

This "Preferred" section asks about tax charges. You must activate the tax option. Margaret Lockhart normally charges the tax, so you must activate it for your company.

Activate tax tracking in QuickBooks:

1. Click "Next" to go to the "Sales tax" screen in the "Preferences" section in the interview.
2. In the "Sales Tax" window, click "Yes" for the question, "Do you collect sales tax from your customers?" Then click "Next."
3. Select "I collect single tax rate paid to a single tax agency."
4. Click "Next."

QuickBooks automatically creates a "liability account," called "Sales Tax Payable," which records tax sales.

5. Complete the information that appears in the "Sale Tax" window as it appears below
6. Click "Next."

Choosing the format of the invoice you want

QuickBooks offers 4 varying formats for invoices: Product "Product," professional "Professional," service "Service," and customized "Custom." The type of invoice you choose affects the appearance.

- ✓ The "Service invoice" is for businesses that provide services, but also sell some merchandise (for example, an interior design firm).
- ✓ The "Custom invoice" is for businesses that find it difficult to have their own designed invoice.

You can also design any of these formats to meet your needs. You will see how that is done in lesson 15 of this guide. For Lockhart Design, which sells mostly consulting services, but also sells an occasional product, we will choose the service invoice format.

Select the invoice format for Lockhart Design:

In the sale of "Invoice Format," leave "Service" selected and click "Next."

Tracking sales orders

If you are using QuickBooks Premier Edition, QuickBooks asks if you want to track sales orders. If so, click "Yes," then click "Next."

But if you are using QuickBooks: Basic or Pro, you will not see these preferences.

Choosing interview preferences

The remaining "Preferences" section is a series of straightforward questions. You just have to click "Yes"/"No," then click "Next" to continue forward in the interview. For this article Do this

Payroll Click "Yes"

Estimates (QuickBooks: Pro and Premier) Click "Yes" Progress invoicing (QuickBooks: Pro and Premier) Click "Yes" Time tracking (QuickBooks: Pro and Premier) Click "Yes."

Type of reports you want to create Select "Accrual-based reports."

Complete the "Preferences" section of the "Easy Step Interview." The only thing left of the "General" section is to specify the starting day.

Selecting a start date When entering your company's financial information, you need to choose a start date in QuickBooks. This is the starting point that you want to use for all of your QuickBooks accounts. The start date is the date in which you give QuickBooks a financial picture of your company's liabilities and assets.

Once you pick on a start date, you enter the transactions of your entire company from that date. That is why you should choose a start date that is not too far in the past for you to handle the information. Many business owners use the previous financial year as their starting dates, such as the end of the last fiscal year, or the last quarter. You need to enter all past transactions from the day after your start date to the present date. For example, If you decide on a date from the beginning of February 29, you will enter your historical transactions from April 1 to today.

Keep clicking "Continue" while scrolling through the "Old Date" section until you see the "Choose Start Date" sale.

Set the starting date:

1. Click, "I want to start filling up comprehensive transactions from here."
2. Enter the Lockhart Design Start Date "12/31/2003"
3. Click "Next"

The General section is complete. Click Next to go to the Revenue and Expense section.

Establish an income and expense account

Since you are an industry selected from the interview above, QuickBooks has created revenue and expense accounts for your company. The "Revenue and Expense" section of the Easy Step interview gives you a pre-determined income and expense account that you can add during the interview.

To complete the Revenue and Expense Account section, do the following:

1. Press "Next" until you see where you need to enter your income account
2. In the "Account name" field, enter "Consultation design" and click "Next"
3. In the "Add another revenue account" sales, select "No"
4. Press "Next" until the "Cost Account" window appears
5. Select "No" instead of "More Details" and press "Next"
6. In the "This is your expense account" window, select "No" for the question "Do you want to add a billing account now?" Click "Next"
7. Click "Next" until you get the "Revenue Details" section

Provide information about your income

In the "Revenue Details" section of the Easy Step interview, you must specify how to track claims, configure items in QuickBooks to track the services you offer or products you sell, and configure supplies (if you plan to track stocks)) in QuickBooks. You need to fill out the Introduction section of the Revenue Details section, as it tells QuickBooks how you need a claim and whether you need financial expenses (for businesses that regularly send account statements).

To complete the revenue sharing section, do the following:

1. In the Revenue Details window, click Next to the Recognition window
2. For the following question: "When you provide a service or sell a product (or on the same day), do you receive the full payment?" Select "Sometimes" and then select "Next."
3. For "Revenue Fees," select "No" and click "Next" until the "Service Items" window appears.
4. In the "Projects" section, click "No" in the three windows and ask if you want to configure "service items," "parts out of stock," "other costs."
5. Press "Next" until the "Revenue Details: Inventory" window appears
6. Click "Next"
7. Click "No" in the "Add Inventory" section.

Enter the opening balance

In the "Opening Balance" section of "Easy Step Interview," you can enter the value that the customer currently owes you, the value you owe to the supplier, and the account balance in the balance statement.

Opening a balance sheet is important because QuickBooks cannot provide you with a true "state of affairs" (your company owes a backlog). An accurate statement of the situation can give you an idea of the financial situation of the company. Also, if you start on the correct balance at a certain date, you can keep your account in QuickBooks according to your bank statements.

Suppose Margaret Lockhart wants to enter an opening balance for her bank account. There are two ways to get a bank account opening balance used by QuickBooks: You can use the final balance of your bank balance before your scheduled start date, or you can use your bank account balance for the latest accounting status prepared by your accountant. Margaret recently had a bank statement, so she will use this method.

To enter the opening balance of your bank account:

1. Read the "Open Balance: Introduction and Information" displayed on the screen, then click "Account" (skip the "Buyer" and "Supplier" options)
2. Press "Next" until the "Credit Card Account" window appears
3. When QuickBooks asks, "Do you want to set up a credit card account," "Credit line," and "Loan and notes payable," click "No."
4. Be sure to respond "Yes" to the question, "Do you want to open a bank account?" And press "Next."
5. Enter "bank" as the account name and click Next.

6. Enter the same date as the Commencement Date (December 31, 2003) for the "Statement End Date."
7. In the "Report balance sheet closing" box, type 8390.00, and then click Next.
8. When QuickBooks asks you to "add another bank account," make sure you answer "No." Then click "Next."
9. For the question "Do you want to print a cheque or place a slip from QuickBooks?", Select "No."

End the interview

The last part of the "Easy Step interview" is "Next Step." This is not an essential part of the initial setup, so we will not cover it in this course.

To leave the Easy Step interview and save your changes, click Leave.

Upon completion of the Easy Step interview, we recommend that you do not use the interview to make changes to your company documents. Instead, make use of the information in the help section described in the next page of this chapter to help you make significant changes and adjustments to your business.

Completing the company configuration process

When setting up your company on QuickBooks, you may need to use the Get Status window to help you set up your company files. The data I have provided here will serve as a guide to the rest of the setup process and help you get started with QuickBooks. To display the Get Status window, select Get Status from the Help menu.

Help with using QuickBooks

QuickBooks offers a wide range of help that you can access in several ways. In case of doubt, QuickBooks will provide:

Hey, come with me for help. This type of assistance exists in the various jobs you do and provides you with information based on relevant information.

Step by step instructions. Use the How-To menu to search your questions and provide you with an index.

Follow me to help

You can find this option in all the operations you perform on QuickBooks and display problems related to what you do. For instance, if you have an invoice form open, you will see support on how to build an invoice using "How do I do it?"

By default, the Tracking Help window is to the left of the QuickBooks workspace. You can move it to any location by dragging it to the desired location.

To open and close the Help-Me window:

To close the Tracking Help window, click k in the upper right corner of the window.

To open the Follow-Me Help window, you must go to the View menu and select Follow-Me Help.

How am I?

With QuickBooks, you'll find a drop-down menu with "How? in the upper right corner of your system. These menus provide easy access to information and instructions for the window being processed. Help topics are usually displayed in the "Follow Me" window.

Use help or F1

The description of most windows can be obtained by pressing the "F1" button. The subject of help is displayed in the "My Tracking for Help" field. Some windows also have a help button. When you click the Help button, help is usually displayed in a separate help window instead of the Follow Me window.

Payment to registered clients

If you receive a payment at the time of sale and the confirmation is complete, QuickBooks will record the payment to the customer. When you bill your invoices and receive them later, you can make payments to QuickBooks in the receipts window.

The receipts window lets you reconcile the fees you receive with the invoices you write. You will use the Receipts window in this lesson.

Receive full payment:

1. In the "Buyer" menu, select "Receipt."

The first phase is to input the name of the customer from whom you will receive the payment.

2. In the "Recipients" field, select "Violette, Mike: Workshop" from the list. QuickBooks shows Mike Violetta's invoice in the "Applies to" section
3. Press "TAB" twice to scroll to "Amount."
4. In the field where you see Amount, type 475.57 and press TAB
5. In the Reference / Cheque Number field, enter 6745 and press TAB
6. In "Pmt. Method", select "Cheque" from the list.
7. If not connected, click "Group with other outstanding funds."
8. Click Save & New

This will record the cost and clear the window so you can enter a new window

Let's take, for example:

Rock Castle Construction received a $1,000 cheque from Ecker Designs, Ecker Designs has two accounts and owes more than $6,000

To enter a partial payment:

1. In the "Recipients" field, select "Ecker Design: Office Repair" from the list. In the middle of the window, QuickBooks will display an invoice. In this case, there are two. Therefore, you must enter the value of the collection in the Amount field.
2. Press TAB twice to scroll to the Amount field and type 1000. Press "TAB" again.

QuickBooks automatically applies Ecker Designs' legacy invoices.

You want to receive this charge on other invoices instead of the oldest invoices. In the Payment column, you can see that the customer has $4,500 credit available.

3. Click on the first "position."
4. Click Set Credit
5. Confirm that $ 4,500 credit is selected, then click Finish

This result will apply to this piece. Note that the "Unused Credit" line is now displayed as 0.00, and the "Unused Pay" line is shown as 4,500.00. We will now apply the rest

$ 4,500 fee the buyer charges to other "businesses."

6. In the Payment column of the first "Deed," change 691.40 to 5191.40 and hit "TAB."

Please note that the Unused Payments and Unused Credit areas are now 0.00

7. Be sure to use "Unused Grouping Assets."
8. Click Save and New

Computation of excess payment

If the buyer sends you an overpayment, simply enter the amount in the "Cash Collection" window, and QuickBooks will track the additional payment. When buyers receive future invoices, you can apply an overpayment on these amounts.

Suppose Rock Castle Construction received a payment of $ 14,300.00 from Pretell Real Estate for "75 Sunset Rd." The bill for this work is $ 14,274.00.

Enter payment:

1. In the "Payment" box in the "Receipt" window, select "Pretell Real Estate: 75 Sunset Rd."

QuickBooks displays invoices as of December 15, 2007, for $14,274.00

2. Press "TAB" twice, then type "14300" in the Amount field
3. Press "TAB" again

QuickBooks filed an "unused payment" of $26.00. QuickBooks will track the amount you pay in excess and can apply it to any future accounts of your customers. The next time you collect and pay a Pretell Real Estate fee, the Receive Payments window will show an unused $ 26.00 credit.

4. Select "Cheque" from the list in "Pmt." Method "
5. Be sure to select "Grouping with other deposited funds."
6. Click "Save & New"
7. When QuickBooks displays a message saying that the customer will receive praise, click "OK."

Collection processing or pre-collection

If the customer pays before they pay for the service, they can receive the payment in the Payment Receipt window. However, since you do not have an invoice to apply for payment, QuickBooks will record the payment slip as an unused payment (just like paying more). QuickBooks retains an unmatched amount of customer name. The next time you register a customer in the Cash Collection window, QuickBooks will display the loan amount in the "Unused Credits" field. The client's condition also reflects the credit line.

Suppose Sonia Bristol wants Rock Castle Construction to make a piece for her. They sent a $1,000 cheque to Rock Castle Construction as a down payment, but the company has not yet paid it.

Payment in advance:

1. In the "Recipients" field, select "Bristol, Sonia: Utilize shed" from the list.
2. In "Pmt. Method", select "Cheque" from the list.
3. Select a number in the Amount field and type "1000". Then press "TAB."
4. If not selected, click "Group with other outstanding funds."
5. Click "Save and Close"
6. When a message is displayed in QuickBooks telling you that the customer will receive praise, click "OK."

Then Rock Castle Construction is ready to prepare the bill, and you have to pay Sonja for the work done by the worker.

Make an invoice for a prepaid customer:

1. In the "Buyer" menu, select "Create Account."
2. In "Customer; Assignment," select "Bristol, Sonia: Utilize Shed" from the list.
3. If you have QuickBooks Premier or Pro, It will display the Available Estimates window. If you do not want to make an invoice from the offer list, click Cancel.
4. Click on the "Project" column, select "Install" from the "Project" list, and then press "TAB."
5. In the "Quantity" column, type "40", then press "TAB."
6. Click Clear Selection
7. In the "Payment" box, type "1000" as the amount to be applied to another invoice, and then press "TAB."
8. In the "amount method," select "Cheque" from the list.
9. Make sure you select "Use other unpaid grouping funds."
10. Click Save and New to register a partial payment and clear the window

Charge a fee for more business

Rock Castle Construction is doing multiple "work" for Brian Cook's buyer. Brian has four notes. He wants the cheque to cover all the bills.

In this exercise, you will apply this simple fee to an invoice with multiple "work."

Filling Multiple Positions:

1. In the "Receipt" window, select Cook from the "Payment" list, Brian

Mr. Cook will pay for all work except the last "kitchen work."

2. Press "TAB" twice to scroll to "Amount."
3. In the "Amount" box, enter "8.626,23" and press "TAB."

Please note that QuickBooks first charges a fee for the earliest accounts.

4. In the "Reference / Cheque" box, type "575", then press "TAB"
5. On the list. Method, select "cheque."
6. Click Save and Close to register the invoice and close the Create Account window

You can now go to the Payments window to see how QuickBooks applies payments to Sonia.

To view your subscription:

1. In the "Buyer" menu, select "Receipt."
2. In the "Recipients" box, select "Bristo, Sonia: Utilize Shed" from the QuickBooks list to enter unused $ 1,000 worth of credits.
3. Click on the "Payment" column and click on "Set Credit."

In the "Discounts and Credits" window, keep in mind that QuickBooks applied for all the credits on the invoice, which is what you want. If you want to apply part of the loan amount to another invoice, you can use this window to apply the credit to the appropriate invoice.

4. Click Finish

QuickBooks applies existing loans to new invoices. Select the demo discount and credit information option to see what happened:

5. Click "Save and Close" to register the points used.

Every other time you receive a payment from Sonia, QuickBooks will introduce her to you.

Deposit

When you use the Enter Bills for Sale window (for cash sales to receive immediately), the Receive Payments window (for credit invoice payments), or payment on the invoice, QuickBooks will track the money received. Come on until you put it in the bank.

Select the payment you'd like to make:

1. In the "Bank" menu, select "Deposit."

2. Make sure to show "Show payment type" as "All types."
3. Click to select the payment you want to send to the bank

In this exercise, select Pretell Real Estate (6,248.73), Mike Violette (1,000.00), Pretell Real Estate (1,200.00), Anton Teschner (3,500.00) and Tuan Nguyen (2,200.00)

4. Click "OK"

QuickBooks displays a "Deposit" window showing the payment you have selected

5. In the "Place in" box, make sure "Cheque" is checked
6. Click "Save and Close" to register your deposit.

How does QuickBooks handle deposits?

QuickBooks has updated its Unallocated Funds account to show you that you have paid in funds. The deposit is simultaneously recorded in the bank account.

To view your Unallocated Funds account:

1. In the List menu, select Chart
2. In the account directory, double-click the Unallocated Funds account.

QuickBooks will schedule your deposit and reduce your account balance by the amount of your deposit

3. Close the "Unallocated Funds" window

You can now see deposit transactions in your bank account.

4. In the account directory, double-click your current account

QuickBooks linked the deposit to a "Cheque" account for the account and updated the balance in your bank account.

5. Close the account registration and directory.

Get deposit money

In the Deposit window, you can enter information about any cash that will be withdrawn from the deposit when registering the deposit.

To register to receive a cash deposit:

1. In the "Bank" menu, select "Deposit."

QuickBooks displays a "Pay Deposit" window. Please note that the deposit for the previous fiscal year is not specified.

2. In the "Payment Deposit" window, select Doug Jacobsen's payment
3. Click "OK"
4. In the "Deposit" window, type "Petty Cash" in the "Return Cash to" box and press "TAB."
5. When QuickBooks shows you a message that reads, "Petty Cash is not on the account list," click on "Settings."
6. Make sure "Bank" is selected from the list and click "OK" to return to the "Deposit" window
7. If QuickBooks asks you to use a computer cheque for this account, click No to continue.
8. In the Cash Return Amount box, type "200", then press "TAB."

QuickBooks displays the subtotal of the deposit ($2000.00) and the total amount minus the refund amount ($1800.00).

9. Click Save and Close

QuickBooks records the total amount of deposits in the Banking account and records the cash in the "Petty Cash" account.

10. To see the performance of these accounts, select Account Overview from the List menu.
11. Close the account directory.

CHAPTER 3: HOW CAN I ENTER CUSTOMER AND VENDOR

Two groups of people help your company succeed: income-generating customers and sellers from whom you purchased goods and services. With QuickBooks, it's easier to get the names of both groups before you start transactions. For both, you can store basic information like addresses, phone numbers, and email addresses, but you can also track almost anything and everything you need to know about your customers and sellers and their hubs. Start with your customers. Note the small icons to the right of each file window for each customer and vendor. A small paper clip is used to attach information, a small pencil to change the information, and the pin shows notes for that customer or seller, as shown here.

Build your client list

You can add your customers to QuickBooks in a variety of ways. You can add them one after another, you can change the menu/add/change/ or if you have saved this information in an Excel sheet or a comma-separated values (.csv) file, you can use a QuickBooks special help to import this information. This import service provide a step-by-step wizard that you can access by running File | select Facilities Import Excel Files. Use the utility to import your vendors, inventory items, and account details. To manually create a new client, click on the Client button on the icon or home page to open the Client Center. Then click on the Client and New Work dropdown arrow at the top of the Client Center window and select New Customer from the submenu. This opens the New Client window. The address information tab in the foreground, then enter the appropriate information.

Customer information

Start with the Customer Name field above. The text you enter here does not appear in printed transactions. You can think of this as an internal code because what you enter in the company's name/full name fields seems like the name of the customer in the printed sales transactions.

Create a customer name system so that you can approach each customer the same way and avoid the risk of entering the same customer several times. For example, if your customer is a company, you can simply enter the business name; if your client is an individual, it is best to enter the family name first into the client name field for sorting purposes. Use the name that you and your staff refer to the customer.

NOTE

Each entry in the Customer Name field must be unique. For example, if you have multiple clients named Titus, be sure to put them in, it's easy to determine which list Titus represents. Because this field can contain up to 41 characters, you should be able to create a handy name system.

Even if QuickBooks uses the open balance field available in New Client Settings with today's date, it is better not to use the open target field. If you enter an amount here, the balance may contain more than one outstanding bill, and you do not have detailed records of what this balance constitutes. This makes it difficult to match payments against specific bills. Because QuickBooks publishes the amount you enter in this field on account requirements and makes a clearing entry into an account called "Opening Balance," at some point, you have to cancel the balance in the "Opening Balance". Entering unique transactions that make the total balance is more accurate than entering a total fund with the opening balance field.

In the Company Name, Full Name, and Address Details fields, enter the company name, contact name if selected, and your billing address. Add another contact information you want to track. If you are sending plant email or invoice data to this customer, be sure to enter your email address.

If the customer has multiple shipping addresses, select a name for each shipping address that is later selected from a drop-down menu when entering sales transactions. If your shipping address is no different than your billing address (or if you never ship products), you can ignore the Ship-To field or click the Copy button to copy data from the bill To field.

To create a shipping address, click the plus button next to the shipping area to enter addresses for the Lead Address Information dialog box. QuickBooks will automatically enter the "Send to 1." Enter the address information, specify whether this address should be the default shipping address, and then click OK. If necessary, enter "Other Ship" to call this customer; he has a default name for "shipping to 2."

Sales tax settings

When you collect sales tax, fill in the fields on that tab. Select the appropriate sales tax code and item for this customer, or create a new sales tax or item here if needed.

Payment settings field

What to sign up for

Account Number: Use this field when assigning account numbers to your customers.

Credit Limit: Set the credit limit to determine the total amount a customer buys from you. If a new order, with all unpaid bills, exceeds the limit, QuickBooks will display a warning.

Even if the warning does not prevent you from selling to the customer, you can send the order (payment on delivery). Also, leaving the credit limit field blank is no different if you go to zero. Zero means that you do not want to sell this loan with credit.

Payment Terms Click the arrow to the right of the Payment Terms field to see a list of predefined QuickBooks terms or select <Add New> to define a new term. The terms and conditions in the list of payment terms are for both customers and sellers, you may need additional requirements to meet your needs.

Price Level: Use price levels to adjust your prices at the customer level. Select an existing price level, or create a new one.

Preferred Delivery Method: This field saves the default value of the way you want to send sales transaction information to this customer, not how products are shipped. Choose None for any particular method, email, or mail.

Preferred Payment Method: Choose from the drop-down menu to indicate which customer prefers to pay or add a new method.

Credit Card Information: Note the credit card information of this customer in these fields. If you choose to store this information, be sure to turn on

QuickBooks customer credit card protection as described in the "Secure Customer Credit Card Information" section later in this chapter.

Online Payments In the Online Payment option shown on the left side of the Payment Settings window, click either credit card or bank transfer to see the Enable Online Payment dialog box, shown in the illustration. Click Yes to subscribe a service to receive a tax.

Payment Options for Customers

If the customer does not pay sales tax, select Not from the Code drop-down menu and enter the customer's reseller certificate number in the "Resale" field.

Additional Information

Use the More Info tab to enter more information about your customers, as described in the following list. Here you can use available fields or create your own custom fields to design reports based on data captured in these fields.

- Customer Map Use this field to sort customers by the type you have chosen, as well as wholesalers and wholesalers. Click the arrow to select a type from the list, or create a new type.
- Rep This field is the place to pursue a salesperson. Seller Representatives may be employees, suppliers, or "other names" as specified in the list of other names. Select a

delegate from the reps list, or add a new delegate by selecting <Add New> from the drop-down menu.

Custom Fields: Custom Fields allows you to create fields to track private information about your clients (such as the contract extension date, for example). Learn how to use these fields in custom fields later in this chapter.

Information Tab Function

You can enter the functionality for this client by selecting the Job Information tab at the right of the new Client Information window. Use the fields on this tab to help you track the state of your work with this client. See the "Using features" section later in this chapter. When filling in the fields, click OK.

Adds different client records

Use the Add / Edit Multiple Lists menu lists to add more clients at once (or to make changes to the information for existing client records). From the Client Center, from the Client and New Works drop-down menu, select Add More Client: Features.

The Add / Edit Multiple Lists window opens with the already selected client list selected. You can add new customers and features, edit customer information, or fill in additional data. You can even copy and paste clients from an Excel sheet into the Add / Edit Multiple List Entries.

To get the best out of the Add / Edit Multiple List Entries windows, note the following important features and functions:

- Filter List and Display Select the View arrow or see only the records with which you want to work.
- Search Field: Use this field to locate and work with a specific client record quickly.
- Personalize the Columns Click to open the Open Columns window where you want to add columns to fields in the client record.
- Copy right-click in any field except the name field and select Copy Down to copy the contents of the selected field to all remaining records in the list.
- Duplicate Row - Set the cursor on each row in the table, right-click, and from the resulting menu, select Duplicate Row to repeat the selected record in the row below. The new duplicate record name starts with "DUP."
- Client Center

QuickBooks stores all of your client information in the QuickBooks Client Center. From here, you can create, edit, and receive customer and job reports. Click the

Client button on the icon or home bar to open the Client Center.

All customer transactions by transaction type are displayed on the transaction tab. Selecting the transaction type shows the current transactions for that type in the right shade. You can manipulate and filter the view by selecting categories and sorting by column.

Personalize client list and features

You can personalize the information displayed in the client list and features. By default, the list has three columns:

- Name
- Total Balance, and
- Appendix.

Client balances appear alongside their names. When you enable the multi-currency feature, the currency column is also visible.

To add more columns to your Customers and Features list, right-click anywhere in the list and select Customize Column to open the Customize Column dialog box, which will appear.

To add a column, select its label in the left pane and click "Add." Alternatively, if you want to delete a column from your list, select its label in the right pane, and click Remove.

Some users add a later column to let them know what customers are billing for or late.

To organize the order from left to right of columns, select a column you want to move, then select Move Up to move a column to the left or move further down Right. The order of the columns displayed in the selected column panel in the dialog box is translated from top to bottom = from left to right.

When you add columns to the clients and features list, you don't see all the information unless you pan the list and expand each column. To maximize this breakdown, click on the Show Full List Only button, the arrow that shows in the upper-right corner of the Customers and Jobs menu.

Works on customer information panel

The Customer Information Panel is where QuickBooks keeps all the customer information you have entered, as well as every sales transaction. You can quickly see the details behind the client's outstanding balance, add or update important notes, or make a specific job, and even run key client reports.

You will see two tabs right on the client center screen. One is the customer list and post; the second is the transaction list. To the right of these tabs is the Customer Information Group. If you do not see this panel, your client list can expand. In this case, click on the left-hand arrow at the far right of the list to show the customer information pane.

The top half of the customer information screen shows basic contact information, along with links to maps, directions, and key reports. The lower half of the shed contains five tabs containing transaction details, contact information, to-do, notes, and email information sent. When working on one of these tabs, click the Manage <Tab Name> button at the bottom of the window to add, edit, or delete the information.

- Transactions: Use the transaction table to filter for information about a particular customer. Choose from different categories in the list. You can add a column of information and right-click anywhere on or under the column headings and select the Personalize column.
- Contacts Use the Contacts tab to store all the ways you can stay in touch with your customers. Click on the drop-down arrows in the available fields, and you will see that there is a place for different types of phone and email information and even social media.

To do From the To-Do tab, click the To-Do button and select Create New to create a specific reminder for that client. This can be very useful because you have to specify the date you want to be remembered (the due field) and, for example, the new To-Do as a call or meeting in the writing field. You can then view the To-

Do note in the calendar or directly in the customer center. When the task is complete, the memory opens and changes its status to Done. Click the Run Reports button on the To-Do tab to see a detailed list of everything you need to do, including those for vendors and employees.

Notes On the Notes tab, click the Manage Notes button to add, edit, or delete a note. The Date / Time Stamp button automatically sets the current date and time when you add text to notepad.

- Send email: This is the best way to track all sales transactions that you have sent to a customer. In a list, you can see the sender of the email, the date it was sent, and the form that was sent, including the reference number and the amount.

Use features

QuickBooks processes clients and functions together, allowing you to create one client and publish all invoices for that client, or create different functions for that client and job level accounts. Some companies just follow the client, but if you are a construction contractor, subcontractor, or service provider based on a project, you have to pursue the tasks. Jobs are not alone; they are always linked to customers, and you can attach as much work to a customer as you need.

When you complete tasks, you can enter all existing functions in the QuickBooks Setup phase or when they start. Because the functionality is related to the client, the client must be present on the list of clients and features and QuickBooks before you can create a job. Once the work is done, you can track the progress and the promised completion date. If you think that this is the only job you do for this client, you can do the same for the client without creating a job because the client record also has the Job Information tab. If you get another project from the client, you can always add this new functionality.

Create jobs

To create a job, open the Client Center, and right-click on the list of clients for whom you are creating a job. Select "Add Job" to open the "New Job" window. Name the task (you can use up to 41 characters) and make them describe enough to understand you and your client. Make any appropriate changes to the Job Title tab. QuickBooks retains this information only for this purpose and will not change the original shipping address in the customer record. Update payment settings and additional information tabs as needed. Sales tax settings are customer-specific rather than functional, so you won't see the Sales Tax Setup tab.

Fill in the details of this function on the Job Information tab. All information in the Job tab is optional. The Job Status drop-down menu offers options that you can change as the task continues. You can change the default text to reflect the way you refer to each level of progress, but the changes you make to the text are system-wide and affect every function. To edit the text, you use to track the status of a function, follow these steps:

Select Edit | Preferences Opens the Preferences dialog.

1. Click on the Job & Estimate icon in the left pane, then open the Company Preferences tab in the right pane to see the current descriptive text for each status level.
2. Change the text of all status levels if you have a descriptive sentence that you like best, such as "work" instead of "in progress."
3. Click "OK" to save the changes; this new text is used in every existing and new function in your system.
4. When you are finished entering all the data related to this task, click "OK" to close the "New Task" window and return to "Client List and Job." The functionality you create for the client becomes part of the client list.

Delete and hide customers and features

Sometimes you need to get rid of a client or a job you created. Deleting a task is more common than deleting clients because sometimes QuickBooks users add a task when estimating a client for a new project and then deleting the task when the project does not materialize.

You can delete a client (or functionality) only if it is not used in a transaction. Although many users complain that they cannot remove a customer who is considered "dead" in their customer list and functionality, unfortunately, there is no equilibrium; the rule in QuickBooks is that you can delete a customer or only delete a function if it is not used No transaction. In addition, you cannot delete a customer who associates at least one functionality. Instead, you must first delete the functionality (if it can be deleted) and then delete the client.

To delete a client or job, select it from the list of clients and jobs and press CTRL-D. QuickBooks will ask you to confirm that you want to delete this client or feature. Click OK to remove the client or functionality. If you have a client that cannot be deleted and is no longer active, you can prevent users from selecting the transaction windows by leaving the client inactive (the client hides so that he does not appear in the drop-down menus). To make a client or a job inactive, right-click its list in the Customers list in Jobs and select Make Client: Job Inactive. If you disable the client, any functionality associated with the client will automatically become inactive. You cannot hide a customer without hiding all the features associated with it.

Active and inactive customers

The list of clients and features is configured to display "Active Customers" (default view), so clients and inactive functions are not shown on the list. To see clients in inactive functionality, select "All Customers" from the drop-down menu at the top of the list of customers and features described below. Clients and inactive features appear with an "X" to the right of their name in the "All Clients" list.

To reactivate a client or function, select "All Customers" as a view, and click "X" next to the client or hidden function to switch back and forth between setup and setup. When you reactivate a client with functionality, QuickBooks asks if you also want to enable all the features. Clicking "Yes" will activate the client in all functions. If you click "No," the client is activated, and all features remain inactive; You can activate each function separately.

Integrated clients or features

Imagine creating a client or job and entering into at least one transaction before realizing that there is a duplicate of an existing client or job for the same client. The best thing to do in this case is to merge client portals or job portals and move the entire transaction log into a client record. Follow these steps to do this:

1. Double-click on the client or work list that you do not want to keep for editing mode.
2. Change the name of the client or work with the name of the client or job you want to keep.
3. Click OK. QuickBooks displays a message telling you that the name is in use and asks if you want to merge the names. Click Yes to complete the merger.

Client merger only works if the client gateway has no functionality associated with it, or if the name of the client you want to delete has no confirmed functionality (it's OK if the name of the client you want to keep has functionality). Merging functions only work if both functions are connected to the same client.

- Use custom fields

You can include your fields and customer, vendor, employee, and item records. Custom fields are useful if you want to track specific information, but QuickBooks doesn't provide a field for them. For example, if you want to renew customer birthdays or yearly contract, you can add fields to track this information. Custom name fields are added to each list of names, but you can configure any field you create to restrict its appearance to specific lists. For example, you can create a custom field that you only want to use for clients in the Jobs list or in both clients, Jobs, and Vendors lists.

Add a custom field

To add one or more custom fields to the names, do the following:

1. Open a center (Customers and Jobs, Providers, or Employees) and double-click on each name in the list to put the record into edit mode.
2. Go to the More Info tab.
3. Click the Select Fields button to open the Set Up Custom Fields for Names dialog box, where you can name the field and point to the list(s) where you want to use the new field.
4. Click OK to save the information. QuickBooks displays a message indicating that you can add these fields to any custom template.

As in other fields, provide secure data in a consistent manner, or the information you receive may not be useful to you when you customize a report to contain this information.

- Secure customer credit card information

When you save customer credit card data, QuickBooks offers security features. These features are designed to help you meet the demands of the payment card industry known as PCI DSS. When you log into your corporate directory as an administrator, you will see a reminder about activating credit card protection when you open the file. The first action you take is to change your administrator password to meet the complex password standards that require credit card protection.

When you save customer credit cards, activate credit card protection as soon as possible. You can perform the task by selecting a company. Protect the customer's credit card and select Enable protection as long as you log on as an administrator user.

The challenge section is mandatory. If you forgot your password, you can click the Reset Password button in the Sign-Up dialog box. If you answer the claim correctly, QuickBooks lets you change your password to a new complex password. When you finish the dialog and click OK, QuickBooks confirms the fact that you changed your password and tells you that you have to repeat this task every 90 days.

Even if you can disable customer credit card protection, this is not recommended when storing your customer's credit card information. To disable this feature, open the Client Credit Card Protection window, select Disable Security, and then respond to the dialog box when you disable it.

QuickBooks protects your customer's credit card

Here are some important points to consider when enabling credit card protection:

- All users with permission to see full credit card details in the client record must set a complex password.

- Password must be changed every 90 days. Users who do not change their passwords cannot open the file. If, as an Administrator user, you do not change your password, the credit card protection feature is turned off, and you will see messages about your failure to comply with specific rules for companies that accept credit cards.
- You cannot re-use any of the last four passwords.
- If the user enters the wrong password three times (sometimes users advise different passwords if they cannot remember their passwords), the user's file will be closed.
- Only Administrator users can configure the features in this feature.
- QuickBooks Credit Card Security Audit Log tracks all transactions with credit cards (including a display of customer credit card information).

View user permissions credit card information

With credit card protection enabled, when users are set up and have full access to sales and accounts, users do not get authorization to view customer credit information unless you specifically select this option. Users who do not have the authorization to view credit card information will only see the last four digits of a credit card. Users who are allowed to see customer information must also create a strong password at the next login.

If you are setting up new users and giving them permission to access customer information, there is no need for a complex password to open them. Provide an easily accessible password, and QuickBooks will change a password when you first log in.

See Security Log

When credit card protection is turned on, QuickBooks keeps a security record called the credit card audit trail. This is a special report that can only be viewed by a QuickBooks Admin user. To open the report, select Reports | Computable

Taxes Check customers' credit card accounts. This report is updated each time a credit card information is entered, displayed, modified, or deleted. Recent activity always appears at the top of the report.

- Make your own sales list

You have the same options when you create the seller list in QuickBooks as you have when you create the customer list. To create a resource, open the Vendor Center from the list of sellers or the main page. Click on the new seller icon at the top of the seller list and select the new seller. As you see how you are managing your customers, a new sales dialog will appear in the Information tab.

Seller information

Start with the resource name field at the top of the window and fill in as much information as you think you need, contacts, phone numbers, etc. The billing of the address block is important if you want to print and verify an email, as this is the email address. If you use window envelopes, if you enter a checkmark in the envelope, the seller's name and address block are selected to display

Window or window. Use the "Shipping by" address if your seller is from a different location than your billing location.

As in the client center, do not enter anything in the opening cell field.

Instead, enter separately the current open sales invoices that represent the current (unpaid) open balances.

Payment settings

Use the Payment Settings tab to store useful information:

- Account number If you have an account number with this seller, enter it here. The number appears in the notepad of printed controls.
- Payment Terms The terms and conditions you enter here apply to all invoices entered for this seller.
- QuickBooks warns you about a credit limit when you submit an invoice that, if added to your current balance, will exceed your credit limit with this seller.
- Invoice Price Level (only available in Premier and Enterprise editions.) If you plan to bill your customers for the work performed by this provider, you can enter either a standard hourly rate or a custom rate here. Each time you create an invoice with billed time, QuickBooks will charge the correct rate for each service item based on the seller who did the work.
- Enter the name when checking by name Fill in this field if the name of the payer is different from the sales name you entered. For example, the seller name for Great State Electric might be "GSE."

Tax settings

If you submit a 1099 form to this seller at the end of the year, enter the tax ID number for that seller and select the Eligible Seller for the 1099 writing box. You will learn more about the 1099 tracking feature later in this chapter.

Account settings

If you select accounts in this window for this seller, they will be displayed automatically when you enter or check a seller invoice. You can always change the pre-filled account before saving or checking the bill, if necessary. You can fill up to three Accounts for the seller, as described below. This feature can be very useful for making loan payments that need a transfer of capital and interest.

Additional Information

Use the More Information tab to include other sales details to improve tracking and reporting:

- Vendor Type Select the vendor type or create one. This field is easy to use if you want to sort sales by type, make reports more efficient.
- Custom Fields You can create custom fields for providers, as well as for custom clients.

Add and edit various sales files

If you want to add information to many or all of the vendor files at once, or you want to find a simple way to integrate new providers in a more streamlined way, use the Add / Edit Multiple List Entries windows.

From the Vendor Center, select New Vendor | Add different sellers. (You can also access this window by selecting / Adding / Adding Multiple List Entries and Selecting Sellers as a List Type.) The menu / Add / Remove List, a Crypto Editor. When the seller was first created, you can even copy and paste sales information from an Excel worksheet into the Add / Modify Multiple List Entries window to create a new sales record quickly.

Here are some important features and features in the Add / Edit Multiple List Input:

- Filter List and Display: Select the view or display arrow only to display the records in your list with which you want to work.
- Customize Column Button: Use this button to open the Columnize windows. Here you can contribute columns to the sales record you want to edit or add columns to fit those in a spreadsheet you want to copy and paste into QuickBooks.
- Copy Down: Right-click any field in the table except the name field, and select the Copy Down command to copy the contents of the selected field to all remaining records in the list.

- Duplicate rows: Right-click on each row in the table and select Duplicate Rows from the context menu that appears to duplicate the selected record in the row below. The new duplicate record name starts with "DUP."
- Sales Center

Your vendor list is stored in the Merchant Center, along with information about each seller's transactions. To open the Vendor Center, select Vendors | Center the seller from the menu bar or click the seller icon on the icon bar. The Vendor Center displays your sales list, gives you quick access to key reports, and makes it easy to enter into vendor transactions.

As with the customer center, the real damage to the vendor center has two tabs: vendor (your vendor list) and transactions. The seller is always selected on the list (by default, the first seller in the list when the Resource Center is first opened), and the left pane of the sales center shows all the details and transactions for the selected seller.

Personalize the seller list

You can customize the information displayed in the seller list as well as the seller information pane on the right side of the window. By default, the seller list has three columns: Name, Total Balance, and Appendix. The Attachment column displays the paper clip icon

73

next to the seller's name when you attach a scanned document or other documents to this record with the Document Center. Use the slider to find the seller you want to see.

Use the drop-down menu at the top of the Vendors tab to see sellers in one of the following ways:

- All vendors
- Active vendors
- Seller with open balances
- Custom filters

Use custom filters to display providers that match the criteria you set in the Custom Filter dialog box. The options in the dialog box are easy to understand and use.

Add more columns to the list by right-clicking anywhere on the list and customizing columns to open the Column Size dialog box. To add a column, select its label in the left pane and click "Add." Returns the information that the column describes for each provider on the list. As long as the seller you are interested in is displayed on the part of the visual list, the information is available - you do not have to select the list or open the record.

You can rearrange the order from left to right for a column by opening the Custom Columns dialog box and selecting the column you want to move. Select Move Up to move a column to the left or Move Down to move it to the right. The order of the columns displayed in the selected column panel in the dialog box is translated from top to bottom = from left to right.

If you add columns to the sales list, you will not see all the information unless you can expand the list panel and adjust the width of each column.

Works in the disguise information section

You can see all the information you enter for each seller and each purchase transaction. Each tab contains detailed information about this seller. Use the Manage <Tab Name> button at the bottom of the window to create a new entry, edit or delete information in each tab. If you do not see the vendor information pane, click on the show list and details arrow on the vendor panel page.

With tabs and filters

Most of the five tabs have one or more filters where you visit your data:

- Transactions The Transactions tab shows all types of sales transactions. There are three filters from which you can organize information. You can sort by any of the five columns by clicking the small arrow to the right of the column layer. You can add, remove, or change columns by right-clicking anywhere in the column headings and clicking "Personalize columns."

- Use the show filter to see all transactions, balance details, and many other options.
- Depending on your selection in the filter, you can use the filter on the option to shorten the displayed results. For example, in the following illustration, bills are selected in the Show Filter, and you can choose from All Bills, Open Bills, or Over Bills.
- Date filters allow you to select the time period for selected information,
- Contacts Use this tab to give more details about who is calling. There are no filters for this option.

To do: Click the To button and select Create New, to create a reminder for a specific resource in the Add To-Do dialog box. View your To-Do note in the calendar or right at the Vendor Center, or click on the Run Reports button to see a detailed list of everything you need to do. There are three filters for this tab: Type, Status, and Date.

Notes: Click the Manage Notes button to add, edit, or delete a note in the Notebook dialog box. Click the Date / Time Stamp Button to automatically enter the current date when text and notebook is added. The only suitable candidate is history.

- Send email Use the Sent Email tab to view and track purchase orders that you send to a seller. As with the Notes option, this is the only available filter date.

Change sales information

Edit the sales information by double-clicking on the sales list in the sales list to open the sales record in edit mode or clicking on the small pencil icon in the sales information panel. Fill in any additional data you need. You can edit any data you enter before. Be careful with changes to the seller name field, but any changes will change as the name appears in the seller list.

Seller reports. The Vendor Name field can also change the name with previous transactions that you deleted in QuickBooks. For example, if your AT&T telephone company changes to Verizon and you change the sales name, all previous cheques and written bill payments to AT&T will appear as written to Verizon.

To open a list of actions, you can do in the seller list, right-click with a click somewhere in the list to see the list here.

Delete or deactivate the seller

You can remove a seller from the list if the seller has not participated in every transaction. To delete a vendor, select its list on the Vendor tab in the Vendor Center and press CTRL-D or right-click its menu to remove the vendor from the context menu. QuickBooks will ask you to confirm that you want to delete the seller; simply click OK to complete the task. If the seller is involved in every transaction, QuickBooks publishes an error message stating that you cannot delete this seller.

If you cannot delete a seller but do not want to use that seller in transactions, you can hide the seller list by disabling it. To do this, right-click on its list in the Vendors list and select "Make Vendor Inactive."

If the seller list is configured to show active providers (default view), inactive providers are not on the list. To see inactive providers, click the small down arrow at the top of the View field at the top of the list and select "All providers" from the drop-down menu. Non-working sellers have an "X" to the left of their lists. To re-enable the seller, select "All Sellers" as a view and click "X" next to the hidden seller

Or function to switch the setting back to active. Inactive sellers are included in the reports, so you can continue to get accurate reports on purchases and other sales activities.

Integrated vendors

By necessarily creating a duplicate resource and entering a transaction, you can merge the vendors and move each transaction history to a single resource record.

Follow these steps:

1. Double-click the seller list you do not want to keep, whose record opens in edit mode.
2. Change the data in the Vendor Name field to match the vendor name match exactly.
3. Click OK. QuickBooks displays a message telling you that the name is in use and asks if you want to merge the names. Click Yes.

Remember to merge the trick is to start with the name of the seller you do not want and merge with the name of the provider you want.

Use custom fields in vendor records

As with the customer list, QuickBooks has the ability to create custom fields only for the seller list. For example, you can create a custom field that you want to use only in the sales list, or in both clients, jobs, and vendor lists.

Add a custom field for merchants

To add one or more custom fields to the Provider List, follow these steps:

1. Open the Vendor Center, select any name in the Vendor list, and then press CTRL-E to put the record into edit mode.
2. Go to the More Info tab.
3. Click the Select Fields button to open the Set Up Custom Fields for Names dialog box where you can create a field name and select the list (s) that use this new field.
4. Click OK to save the information. You will see a message reminding you that you can add this new field to any custom template.
5. The Additional Info tab shows each name in the list (s) you have selected for the field, and you can add data to each name with which the field is associated. Enter data in a consistent way so that you receive accurate information when you customize reports that contain that information.

- Create 1099 vendors

QuickBooks only supports the 1099-MISC model. If sellers are willing to report 1099, provide this information when preparing them.

Make sure that the QuickBooks file is set up to track and process 1099 forms. Select Edit | Preferences, click on the tax icon: 1099, and go to the Company Preferences tab to see your preferences. Click Yes Next to Question Are you getting 1099-MISC forms? You must complete a 1099-MISC form at the end of the calendar year for a seller who has paid $ 600 or more for services and whose business is an individual or partnership.

To complete Form 1099, you must have a Sales Tax Identification Number (TIN), which can be a Social Security Number or an Employer Identification Number (EIN). Open any matching vendor list and open the Sales Tax Settings tab. Select the option labeled Sales Seller for 1099, and fill in the VAT ID number.

CHAPTER 4: ENTRY AND PAYMENT OF BILLS

Account Processing in QuickBooks

When there is a business expense, it can be managed in one of the following ways:

You can manually write a cheque and then enter the information later in the QuickBooks checklist. This does not take advantage of QuickBooks, but it is sometimes required. For example, if you buy a retail source, they pay immediately, and you cannot know the amount in advance.

Cheques - You can write and print cheques using QuickBooks. When you receive an instant payment invoice, you can write your QuickBooks cheque faster and more accurately than manually, and you get an added bonus: QuickBooks hold items in your checking account.

Paying bills with QuickBooks

Some business owners, especially smaller ones, pay the bills when they receive the bills. However, it is easier for most business owners to pay smaller bills. (They also want to keep money with the company for as long as possible.) If you do not plan to pay your bills immediately, QuickBooks can help you keep track of delays and arrears.

The money you owe on your unpaid account is called collectible. QuickBooks uses paid accounts to track the money you owe. As with any QuickBooks balance account, a paid account has a record in which you can view all your accounts instantly.

To view your debt records:

1. In the Menu list, select Character List
2. Double-click "Payable Accounts" in the list to open the registry.

The registry won't forget every account you enter, it won't show an expiration date, and it will balance you with all your balances. As a business owner, this helps you predict your cash flow and helps QuickBooks remind the system in time to pay.

3. Press "ESC" twice to close the open window.

Paying a bill with a bill-paying bill involves two steps: entering a bill and paying a bill. You will practice these two steps in this course.

When you receive an invoice from a vendor, you should connect it to QuickBooks as soon as possible. This updates the cash flow forecasting report and does not give you the opportunity to forget your account.

Rock Castle Construction received an invoice from the company that created the new booklet. This bill includes courier fees. Rock Castle Construction plans not to pay the bills by the deadline, but the company wants to monitor the total amount of debt paid, so the bill is now merged.

Enter account:

1. In the "Suppliers" menu, select "Enter Billing."

In the upper half of the window is your account. The bottom half is an information area where you can allocate the sum to another Cat account, customer or company.

Note that the cheque box receives a checkmark. The only time you have received an order that has to clear the checkbox is if you use QuickBooks for inventory and want to register the item received, but you have not actually sent the invoice.

2. In the vendor field, type Villas Advertising and press TAB
3. In the "Amount due" box, type "1500."
4. Click on the "Billing accounts" field

Please note that QuickBooks gives you a date in the "Billing Accounts" field. The date showed is 10 days from the date in the Date field. You can change the date as needed. If your vendor list includes built-in vendor payment terms, QuickBooks uses these criteria to calculate its expiration date.

6. Click "Account" in the "Charges" column and enter "Print."

Quick Fill interrupts entry and displays printing and copying of your account. QuickBooks allows you to assign transactions to multiple accounts so you can track

A place where your company spends money. Rock Castle Construction wants to allocate most of this bill to the cost of printing and copying, while the rest is allocated to the bill for freight costs.

5. Press "TAB" to accept "Print & Copy" as your order
6. In the "Taxes" list, select "Not used" and press "TAB." (We ignored the tax on this transaction). Press "TAB" again.
7. Enter "1450" to change the amount from 1,500 to 1,450
8. Click the "Account" column under "Print & Copy"
9. Select "Delivery and Delivery" from the list and press "TAB."
10. In the "Taxes" list, select "Not used" and press "TAB."

QuickBooks automatically assigns the remaining invoice value ($50.00) to "upload and deliver."

11. Click "Save and Close" to register the invoice

When you start QuickBooks or open a file from QuickBooks, a window will pop up, alerting you if you need to complete some transactions, such as an account that must be paid or money saved.

Tip: If you do not see the reminder window when you start QuickBooks, you can activate it by selecting Preferences from the Edit menu.

Click the Reminder icon in the left menu, click the My Favorites tab, and select View Alert List when opening companies.

When QuickBooks tells you that you are late, you can display the Billing Accounts window and select the account you want to pay.

Pay your invoice:

1. In the "Vendors" menu, select "Pay bills."

The payment window displays invoices that have not been paid since the date you entered. You can pay by cheque and credit card.

2. In the "Payment Method," select "Print."

Selecting this option will tell QuickBooks to print this cheque later.

3. Select the Villas Advertising invoice by clicking the column to the left of the account.

QuickBooks display a checkmark next to the account and change the amount in the bank's "Final Balance" to reflect a $ 1,500.00 payment. If you want a partial payment, you can enter the amount you want to pay into the amount. Pay. "

4. Click Pay & Close

How QuickBooks records payments to your account

When you make a payment through the Billing Payment window, QuickBooks enters the Payables record, showing a total reduction of $ 1500 in the account. Also, make a cheque from your "bank" account to pay the bill.

To view the entries in your debt records, do the following:

1. In the Company menu, select Book Chart
2. In the account directory, double-click the "Supplier Balance" account
3. Close the Vendor Accounts Register

While QuickBooks registered entry in his debt record, he made his entry on his cheque account.

Entries:

1. In the account directory, double-click "Cheque."

Please note that the third last digit in the register is the one used to pay for Villas Advertising.

2. Select the "Villas Advertising" transaction

QuickBooks highlight the Villas thick-ribbon transaction, indicating that it has been selected.

3. In the toolbar, click "Edit Transaction."

This cheque is called a "periodic cheque" and is different from the form of the cheque you use to enter a cheque directly into your checking account. (The form shows the fee directly on the cheque portion, and the bill payment form shows the bill paid by cheque.)

4. Press "Esc" to close the "Payment Cheque" window.
5. Close all QuickBooks windows from the Windows menu options. If it asks if you will like to save the transaction, select "No."

Apply vendor discounts to account payments

If you use an early payment discount from some vendors, you can register for the discount directly in the cheque out the window. You can install QuickBooks to track discount amounts.

In this section, you will receive an early payment quote from Rock Castle Construction.

Apply discounts to instant payments:

1. In the "Vendors" menu, select "Pay bills."
2. In the "Expiration or Win" box, type "1/16/08" and press "TAB."
3. If necessary, select "Discount Date" from the "Sort By" list.
4. Click to mark Hamlin Metal invoice with effective date 10/1/08
5. Click on "Set Discount"
6. QuickBooks displays a "Discounts and Credits" window containing information about Hamlin Metal Suppliers' terms and discounts based on these terms (in this case 2% of $ 770.50 or $ 15.41)
7. In the "Discount Accounts" list, select "Structure: Discounts Received" to track the value of the discount.
8. Click Finish

The "Payment order" window will be displayed with the amount of "Hamlin metal" payable minus the discount:

9. Click "Pay & Close"

Note: You can install QuickBooks to always use vendor discounts and bonuses. If you always register a vendor discount in the same account, you can install a default account. In the Edit menu, select Preferred. Click Purchases & vendors, and then click the Preferred Companies tab. Select "Automatically use discounts and credits" and then select the account you want QuickBooks to track the discounts you get from your vendor.

CHAPTER 5: BANK ACCOUNT AND RECORDS

How to write a cheque

When you write a cheque in QuickBooks, you can see the address information and easily split the cheque between multiple accounts.

Let's say you have to write a cheque to pay your phone bill at Rock Castle Construction.

To write a cheque:

1. In the "Bank" menu, select "Write Cheque."

The Bank Account section shows the account you write this cheque. QuickBooks will display the current date in the date field. You may adjust any of these values as needed, but they are suitable for our example.

2. Select the "Print" option
3. In the "Pay by account" box, type "Call Phone."

If QuickBooks notifies you that you have opened an account for this seller, press OK. You get this reminder because you should never use the Writing Cheque window to pay the bills you entered earlier than QuickBooks.

4. Press "TAB" to move between fields.
5. Enter 156.91 (phone bill value) and press "TAB."
6. Click the "Accounts" tab on the "Charges" tab and select "Utilities: Phone" from the list

On the "Cost" tab, you can assign a cheque amount to one of the expense accounts in the Company account directory. In this case, Rock Castle Construction assigns a cheque to its sub-accounts for utilities and phones. Use the Projects tab only when purchasing items that are scheduled to be in stock. Please note that the amount is deducted from the feline amount, and tax is shown separately.

7. Click Save and Close
8. In the "Bank" menu, select "Use registration."

Rock Castle Construction has several types of bank accounts, so QuickBooks will display a "Use Registration" window and ask you to specify the required account.

9. Click "OK" to accept the cheque as the order you want to view.

Please note that the cheque you just wrote is listed in the registry as a cheque that needs to be printed.

10. Close the Registered Cheque Account

How to make use of bank account records

When working on QuickBooks, you usually use forms, cheques, or invoices to enter information. But in the background, QuickBooks records your entries in the appropriate account records. Each account in the balance sheet is listed in the account directory associated with it.

Open the record

When the QuickBooks form appears on the screen, you can see the account registration by selecting Use Registration from the banking menu or by double-clicking the account name in the account directory.

Open the record (when opening the form):

1. In the List menu, select Chart
2. Double-click the savings account in the account directory

Common features of QuickBooks records

All QuickBooks records do the same, regardless of the account associated with them. The following are some common features of all QuickBooks records:

1. The record shows each transaction that affects the account balance and displays them in chronological order (but you can change the order by selecting other category options for the

93

drop-down list). For example, a bank account contains a cheque you wrote (or using QuickBooks or a manual), deposited into the account, and the money you received from the account.

2. The columns in the record provide specific information about the transaction. The first column is the date. The second column shows the reference number (cheque number or vendor postal code) and type (for example, indicates whether the transaction is in the name of a cheque or bill payment). The following column lists the payee, the account to which the transaction was assigned, and any descriptive comments you choose to make. The last column of your bank account shows the amount of the transaction (or in the "Payment or Deposit" column) and whether the transaction closed the bank (indicated by a checkmark in this column).

3. In each transaction line, QuickBooks will display the current account balance. The bottom of the registration window shows the balance of the account closure - the balance takes into account all transactions connected to the register, including cheques that are not printed.

To complete this exercise:

1. Close the Save Miker window
2. Close the account directory

Entering a cheque manually

Sometimes you may have to write a cheque on the spot. QuickBooks allows you to write a cheque and then later enter a cheque into your bank account or cheque form.

Suppose you pick supplies one day, stop by the bookstore and find a new office chair for $ 99.95. The sale is up to date, so you write a cheque on the spot. You must register it later at QuickBooks.

To manually enter a cheque into your bank account register, do the following:

1. In the "Bank" menu, select "Use registration."
2. Click "OK" to accept "Cheque."
3. Click the Number in blank transaction field at the bottom of the record and double-click to select a number.
4. Type 1204 and press "TAB."
5. In the "Payment, type Bayshore Office Supply" box, press "TAB."

A message appears on QuickBooks saying "Bayshore Office Supply" is not a "name list."

6. Click on "Quick Add"

QuickBooks displays the Select Name Type window

Bayshore Office Supply is a "supplier," so you accept the options shown.

7. Click "OK," and QuickBooks adds a new vendor to the "Vendor List."
8. In the "Payment" box, type 99.95 and then click the "TAB" button
9. In the "Notes" box, type "office chair."
10. The "Cheque" account must be displayed this way.
11. Click on "Save"
12. Close the Registered Cheque Account

Transfer between accounts

You can easily register whether you have transferred funds from your financial institution's account using the QuickBooks Transfer Funds option. Rock Castle Construction wants to record that a cheque for $5,000.00 was passed on to savings.

Remittance:

1. In the "Bank" menu, select "Funds transfer."

Please note that QuickBooks displays the current balance of your "Cheque" account.

2. In the "Funds Transfer to" field, select "Savings" from the list.
3. In the "Transfer Amount" box, type 5000.00 and press "TAB."
4. Click Save and Close

QuickBooks reduces the balance on a "cheque" account by $ 5,000, and the balance on a "savings" account by $ 5,000.

Reconciliation of Bank Account

Reconciliation is done to make sure your bank account matches your bank records.

Reconciliation statement

When you use QuickBooks to save your records, you don't have to worry about compile or subtraction errors like you would with QuickBooks.

Use paper records. Nevertheless, it is important to develop the habit of reconciling your QuickBooks account every month. This can help you avoid cost overruns for checking cheques, giving you the ability to find possible banking errors and help you keep more accurate financial records. The bank will send you a statement from each account on a monthly basis. This statement shows all activities in your account since the last statement:

When you receive a statement from a bank or credit card company, you must keep your statement in accordance with the QuickBooks recording. You can easily cross-check in case there are any discrepancies between your bank record and QuickBooks records, including savings fund accounts and market values. The purpose of reconciliation is to ensure that your QuickBooks records and account statements are in line with your account balance.

To reconcile, do the following:

1. In the "Bank" menu, select "Reconciliation."
2. In the "Account" field, be sure to select "Cheque."
3. In the "Final Balance" box, type 106,803.13
4. In the "Service Fee" box, enter 14.00
5. In the "Service Costs" field, select "Banking Fee" from the list.
6. Click "Continue"
7. In the Cheque, Payment, and Services section, select Cheque 265 worth $ 1,200.00 from Reies Properties and cheque 266 worth $ 2700.00 from Larson Flooring.
8. In the "Deposits and Other Deposits" section, select "Check # 9" deposit from 07/10/10 for $109.25.
9. Click "Reconciliation Now"
10. In the Reconciliation Report Report window, select Details, and then click View.

Because QuickBooks Pro and QuickBooks Basic only store the latest compliance, if you plan to re-print the compliance report, you'll need to print them to a file. QuickBooks overwrites previous reconciliation reports with the latest reconciliation data.

If you use QuickBooks Premier, you can print your previous reconciliation report.

In addition, if you are using QuickBooks Premier, there are two additional options for the report: Reconciliation Difference Report and Reconciliation Summary. The Reconciliation Differences report lists change transactions since the last reconciliation. This report is useful when the QuickBooks Balance Sheet Certificate differs from the balance of the last account statement for the previous period. The Summary Reconciliation Report gives a quick overview of deposits/loans and total cheques/payments during the reconciliation period.

11. Close the Report window

Now that you know that the balance in the bank records at QuickBooks, the last bank balance is true. The next time you review your bank records, you'll see a checkmark in the deleted column next to each reconciliation transaction.

CHAPTER 6: PAYROLL

Set Time Tracking

QuickBooks may have already set up time tracking features for you, depending on your answers when setting up your company. To see if time tracking is enabled, select Edit | Preferences from the QuickBooks menu bar. Choose time and Expenses by scrolling to the last category in the left panel and clicking on the Company Preferences tab. Make sure the Yes option is selected.

By default, QuickBooks assumes that your work week starts on Monday. However, some companies use a different workweek, such as Sunday through Saturday, to track downtime. If you are pursuing employee time and the intention of having pay plans, make sure your workweek matches the days covered by your pay period.

QuickBooks has two-time tracking options: a weekly schedule and a schedule on which you can enter an activity. To see them, click Enter Time on the Home screen, or from the menu bar, click Enter Time.

Add time tracker

You can track the time for your employees or external contractors (suppliers) or yourself. Anyone who has to track their time first must exist in QuickBooks and of course, fill in a schedule.

Use the QuickBooks Weekly Timesheet to enter daily tasks for all employees.

If you created QuickBooks Pay when you first set up your company, you may already have QuickBooks employees, and you can use schedules to track their time. You can create a payday from the data entered into each schedule. But for this to work, you need to change the employee record as follows:

1. Selection of Personnel | Employee Center To open the Employee Center, click the Employee Tab to see the list of employees.
2. Select the employee for whom you want to use time tracking.
3. Click on the Edit button to open the Edit Employee dialog box. You can also right-click the employee name in the employee list and select Edit Employee.

From the Edit Employee dialog box, select the Pay Information tab. At the bottom of the income range, select the "Use time data to generate paychecks" at the bottom right. Click OK.

If you need to track employee time to create job reports or a client invoice, you can use QuickBooks schedule without time data to generate paychecks. In this case, make sure that the box "Use time data to create paychecks." Even if you do not use QuickBooks in your payment, you can create staff in the Staff Center to track time and use timeline data for the external payroll service.

Track the time of the sale

Any vendor in your system who pays you or keeps track of their time can follow this time, thus billing your customers. These providers are often outside contractors or subcontractors. To bill customers, just note the time in a timeline and select "Billable hours."

Track the time of other workers

If you need to track down the time of people who are not employees or vendors, use the list with other names. For example, if you are paying employees who use Payrolls and QuickBooks, but you make a drawing instead of a paycheck, add your name to the other name list to track your time. If your company is a property or partnership and you have no employees, enter the owner or partner's name in the list of other names to track time.

Add tasks

There are already many tasks that you perform in your system plan as service items that you use when billing customers for services. However, because you can use time tracking to analyze how people in your organization spend their time, you may want to add service items that do not have to do with the tasks that clients perform.

For example, if you want to track the time people spend on administrative tasks, add a service item named Administrative to your list of items. You can be more specific by naming the specific administrative tasks you want to track, such as accounting, equipment repair, etc. To enter new items, select Menus | List items from the menu bar. Press CTRL-N to open the New Item dialog box. Select Service as an item, where only service items and timesheets are tracked, and name their new item.

- When you perform administrative tasks, create a service called Administration, and make each specific administrative task a management subtitle.
- Do not add an amount to the price box. You can enter the amount when making a payment (via payment check or check payment).
- Because QuickBooks wants to register an account for a service, choose a "fake" (or placeholder) recovery account, such as other revenue or time tracking revenue. No money has ever been posted to the account because you did not sell these services directly to customers.

- Works with airplane

QuickBooks has two ways of recording time for tasks: an individual activity and a weekly schedule. An individual activity is a form you use to accomplish what you did as you performed a task at a particular time on a specific date. For example, a single activity model may note the fact that you are making a phone call on behalf of a customer, repairing equipment for a customer, or performing certain administrative tasks for the company.

A weekly schedule is a template that shows the amount of time and date a person worked in a particular week. All the schedule entry may also contain the name of the client for whom the job was done. You can also print a blank schedule that an employee can fill out and use to enter QuickBooks once a week at a time.

Adjust the format to show the time

If you run time and timesheet models, you can use the minute format (hh:mm) or decimal format (6.5). To reach a default, select Edit | In the General category, select the Company Preferences tab. Use the options in the Time Format section of the dialog box to select the format you prefer. If you set the preference to a decimal number and enter the time as 1:30 when you press TAB to move to the next field, QuickBooks changes the entry to 1.50 (or the other direction if you select minutes). The following message appears when the Individual Activity Time option is selected to remind you.

Track an activity

To track a single event or task with an individual activity form, select Employees | Indicate time / Enter an activity. To track time in each activity, click the Start button in the Time / Enter Individual Activity Window Duration box when the task begins. To pause the account, press pause, when paused. Then, click Start to pick where you left off. To turn off the timing, click Stop. Create due time. The stopwatch always shows the time in (hh: mm: ss) format. If you set your format preferences to a decimal number, QuickBooks will convert the time the stopwatch is off.

Fill in the following fields:

- The default date is the current date. Even if you change the date to an earlier date, you cannot change the date when you use the stopwatch.
- Name Select a name from the Vendors, Employees, and Other Names drop-down menu.
- Client: Select the client or job, even if the client does not have an invoice.
- Service Element - Select the item from the drop-down menu and enter the amount of time in the Duration box.

- Payment component If available, select the payment element that applies to this time. This only appears when the employee is connected to time tracking.
- Class When you activate your classes, select the class from the drop-down menu. If you link an employee to the Time Tracking system, and you also enable Chapter Tracking, the chapter field will not work unless you enable the Revenue Item option in Payroll and Employee Preferences.
- Note Enter any appropriate information. You can pass these notes on both bills and business reports.

When the activity form is complete, click Save & New to fill in another individual activity form, or click Save & Close to finish. A "Stopwatch on" message appears asking if you want to stop the timer, as shown here.

Use of weekly schedule

The weekly schedule records the same information as the individual activity form, except that the information is recorded every time in the weekly blocks, and you have the opportunity to enter the same time information and batches for both employees and non-employees.

To use the weekly schedule template, select Employees | Make the time to use the weekly schedule. Use the following instructions to fill the schedule.

1. In the Name field, select either an individual employee or a sales name from the drop-down menu. Optionally, select either Multiple Names (Payroll) or Multiple Names (Non-Payroll) listed at the top of the list below, as described below, to create more timelines with the same information about the names you use in your Selected list. This last option is useful if you have a team of employees or contracts working on the same project and doing the same work for the week.
2. By default, the form will open in the current week. Click the calendar icon if you need to choose another week.
3. In the Customer: Job column, select the client or job related to the activity.
4. In the Service column, select the appropriate service item.
5. For the employee whose salary is attached to the airplane, use the "Payments" column to determine which payroll is appropriate for the activity. (If the name in the name field is not an employee whose salary is linked to schedules, the "Payroll" column will disappear.)
6. In the Notes column, enter all necessary notes or comments.

7. Click the column that represents the day of the activity, and enter the number of hours worked in the task. Repeat throughout the week for each day that the same activity was done for the same client or job. The total hours entered were shown in the Total column.
8. Go to the beginning of the next line to assign another activity or the same activity to another client, repeat this procedure until the weekly schedule is filled.
9. For each line, indicate whether the time in the billable column is inexpensive. Click the checkbox to remove the checkmark in the invoice column if the time in this line is not invoiced. QuickBooks lists all the time entries associated with the customers.
10. Click "Save" and "New" to create a schedule for another week. When you are finished, click Save and Close.

You can copy the schedule for the previous week by clicking on the "Copy Last Sheet" button after entering the current date in the "Schedule" window and selecting a name. This is useful for workers who have similar schedules of data every week. This description

Applies often to your office staff or to external contractors who do large jobs that last a few weeks. For some employees who usually work for the office and a client is not charged, the schedule may be the same from week to week.

- Information planning report

Before using the information in your client invoice or paycheck, you must transcend the data in your schedule reports. You can view and customize reports, edit information, and print original schedules.

Run scheduled reports

To run reports and timesheets, select Reports | Functions, time, and kilometers. The following reports provide time tracking information:

- Time by Job Summary shows how much time each service spends on customers and work.
- Time-by-Job Details Shows details of the time spent by each client and job, including dates and whether the time is billed. A

The status of unpaid invoices shows that the time is billable but has not yet been used on the customer invoice.

- Time by name shows the amount of time each user tracks.
- Time By Item shows an analysis of the time spent on each service your company spends, including customers you have made.

Change entries in a report

When you browse the report, you can double-click on an activity list to jump to the original entry. You can make changes to the original entry, such as selecting or deleting the f-invoiced option or change the note field by contributing a note or changing the contents of the current note. Before using the customer or payment plans, be sure to review them and make corrections. In fact, you want to take this step before looking at any of the job, time, and mileage reports.

The most common review is the removable status. If there are contractors or outside employees who fill out schedules, it is not uncommon for some confusion about clients receiving bills in real-time. In fact, you may have clients who are billed directly on only some of the activities and offer the remaining activities as part of your core services.

To review timesheets, open a new weekly schedule, and enter the name of the person connected to the schedule you want to view.

From the Timeline window, or use the calendar icon to navigate to the timeline you want to review. Then, change the information as needed. If necessary, adjust the number of hours for each activity item, change the status of the invoice, and view (and change, if necessary) any notes. If you have already used the timetable data to create an invoice for the customer

Or for the employee to pay, any changes you make to the schedule will not automatically update these documents.

Print weekly tables

Employees often print their weekly schedule and deliver it to those responsible for monitoring and managing staff hours. Often this is the same person doing the payment activities. To print timesheets, select File | Print Shape Timelines from the QuickBooks menu bar to open the Select Timelines window. In this window, you can:

- Change the date range to fit the schedules you want to print.
- By default, all planes are selected. To remove a schedule, select its list and click on the column with a checkmark to turn off this list. You can click on Select None to select all lists and then select a checkmark for one or more users.
- To print notes in full, select the option Three activity notes. Otherwise, the default choice is to print only the first line of each note.

The Select Print Timelines dialog box contains a Preview button, and clicking on it shows a print preview of the selected timelines. When you click on the Print button in the Preview window, timesheets are sent directly to the printer, so you do not get a chance to change the printer or any print width. Clicking the Close button in the Preview window brings you back to the Select Print Timelines dialog box.

Click OK to open the Print Timesheets window where you can edit printers or print options. You need to change the number of copies to print to fit the number of people you are distributing schedules to, Note the last column that indicates your billing status. The entries are symbols as follows:

- B invoice but no invoice for the customer yet
- Unreadable
- D invoices and invoices already for the customer

Customer bills for the time

If you enter time and mark it as billable and check it for accuracy, it is easy to bill your customer directly from the Create Invoice window. From the "Create Factures" home page, select the client's name from the "Job: Job" drop-down menu. The first time you select a client with a schedule change, QuickBooks displays a message telling you that the customer or feature you selected has an appointment to receive the bill, as described later. You are either asked to specify the time for the bill (as well as the cost) to add to your bill or exclude the time and cost and now leave it for the bill later. You can also provide QuickBooks to save your choice by clicking the Save This As A Preferences checkbox.

When you select the option to add billing technology to the invoice, QuickBooks displays a "Choose billable time and invoices" window. Select the Time tab to see all the uninterrupted time that this client or job has been assigned. Click on Select All.

View your bill from your customers all the time that appears in this window, or place a checkmark next to the hours you just want to bill.

By default, each entry with a different service item will appear as a separate item on the invoice. To merge the clock for all items in this window as a single item in the invoice print (the detailed view is still displayed on your screen), check the "Selected time and cost as a single invoice" box above the window. Clicking on the options button gives you additional ways to customize how the information from the airplane contains your bills.

Mileage Tracking

You can use QuickBooks to track a mile of vehicles, as shown below. You can use mileage information to keep track of expenses associated with the vehicle

Mileage as part of the effort to estimate labor costs, estimate customers for mileage costs or keep records of vehicle reduction. Your accountant could use the vehicle mileage data for your income tax return. You can either deduct your actual mileage or other vehicle costs; you cannot deduct both. Your accountant, who works with the numbers you provide as a result of mile tracking, will make the decision.

To track a car, you must first add the car to your vehicle list. Once the vehicle is in your QuickBooks system, you can start mileage.

Enter mileage rates

To track mileage costs, make sure you have correct mileage rates in your system. These changes change frequently, so you should stick with the latest IRS numbers. QuickBooks calculates the cost of miles based on the information you enter. To get the current rate, check the IRS (www.irs.gov), or ask your accountant. To enter mileage for your use, follow these steps:

1. Select Company | Enter vehicle miles to open the Vehicle Distance dialog box.
2. Click the Mileage Rate button on the toolbar to open the Multiple Rate Rates dialog box.
3. Select a date from the calendar as the effective date.
4. Enter the IRS rate for that date.
5. Click Close.
6. Close the Vehicle Distance dialog box (unless you use it to enter miles).
7. The Mileage Dialogs accept different dates and dates. When tracking mileage, QuickBooks uses

the appropriate rate, based on the mileage input date, to calculate costs.

Create a mileage point

When billing customers for mileage, you should create an item (called Mileage, Travel, or something similar). The item you create can be either a service type or a different fee.

- If you want your customers for miles as reimbursable costs and consider them as revenue, use the line item "Other Costs" and select the option "This item is used in things or an affordable cost." Then enter the corresponding expenses in income accounts.

It is important to understand that the Mileage you enter in the Mileage Dialog will not automatically be displayed on the item you created for Mileage. Therefore, you must manually fill in and update the article rate when the IRS rates change. You can use the same rate you use in the Mileage Dialog, or enter a different rate to create a tag - or even a discount if you like.

Miles entrance

After configuring your mileage company file, you can track mileage in the Enter Mileage Vehicle dialog:

1. Select Company | Track your car mileage.
2. Select the appropriate car from the drop-down menu in the field and enter the following data:

- Due date.
- Distance readings (QuickBooks calculates the total mileage for you). You can reject crash messages and manually enter miles, but entering the phone numbers creates a stream of reports closer to what the IRS auditor wants to see (the IRS likes "records" that contain crash measurements).
- If you want to reject your customer for miles, click on the "bill" box and select the customer: the work and item you traveled for the distance and the category (if you are tracking chapters).
- If you do not want to invoice a customer but want to track the labor costs, choose the client: Job, but do not see the opportunity "invoice."

You can add mileage costs to the customer invoices in the same way as the time charges.

Create mileage reports

QuickBooks contains four mileage reports that are in | Reports include functions, time, and kilometers. Select the submenu report. When working in the "Enter the distance travel" dialog, reports are available in the drop-down menu when you click the arrow next to the Mileage Reports button at the top of the dialog box.

Explanatory report

Vehicle Mileage Follow this report for each file interface to calculate the total mileage and mileage for each vehicle you are tracking.

Mileage with Vehicle Details View details about each mileage entry you have created. For each vehicle, the report calculates the end date of the trip, total mileage, mileage, and mileage. Customer information does not appear in the report, but you can double-click on each listing to record the original mileage entry to see if it is a bill or pay a feature.

Mileage Summary per Job View total number of miles connected to customers or jobs. The report shows the total miles for each customer or job for which you entered an item and shows the billable amount for each mile of entries that you have specified for invoice.

Mileage per job details Information about each trip for each client or job. The report includes the expiry date, invoice status, article, total mileage, sales price, and amount.

Auto mileage reports

- Payment preparation

Now that you understand how to track QuickBooks for hours, you can process your payment through QuickBooks, as this section explains. If you have not yet set up your payment, check with your accountant for advice on choosing the payment option that best fits your business needs and ensure that your setup is fully compliant with state and local tax authorities.

QuickBooks Desktop Payroll Services

QuickBooks offers a variety of payment services designed to work with your company data. Each service requires a separate charge for Intuit. Here is a brief summary of what is currently available:

- Basic payment provides tax tables and automatic calculations of salary reductions and employer costs for up to three employees. Tax forms are not included, so you either have to work with your accountant on tax filings or manually adjust your tax forms. QuickBooks makes it easy to manually set up tax forms by submitting detailed reports in Excel.
- Improved payment adds tax forms and electronic records to both federal and state reports.
- Full Payment Transfer the task of managing your payment, withdrawing holdings, paying employer contributions, printing government forms, and submitting them to QuickBooks. All

you have to do is enter the work hours of your employees.

Additional plans are available, such as the Intuit online payment service, which does not require the use of QuickBooks for your accountability, and improved payroll for accountants, which allows you to set up payroll for up to 50 companies (including reparation of federal models and state levels), including the ability to enter payroll data according to The Fact. If you are looking for a complete solution, consider the Full-Service option - you enter your employees' time, and Intuit manages the rest.

Activate the QuickBooks Detection Service

When you start, make sure you enable the full payroll feature in your QuickBooks company file by editing | Preferred Salaries and Employees Company Preferences

| Full salaries. Selecting this option enables the employee payment information fields and adds the Run On button in the Employee section of the QuickBooks home page. Click the Play On Payroll button to identify and subscribe to a QuickBooks menu offer.

When the registration process is complete, download the files you need to operate the payment.

New files are automatically added to your QuickBooks system; you don't have to do anything to install them. In addition to the payroll program, the current tax table is added to your system. After the payment is installed, the employee list contains all the orders you need to have the payroll.

Make your payment manually in QuickBooks

If you only have one or two employees, you can choose to run manual payrolls at QuickBooks. Remember that if you process your payment manually, no deduction or tax is automatically calculated for each paycheck you create; You need to sign up for a QuickBooks payroll service. You can use the IRS Employer Circuit E, calculate expenses, and enter them manually when you create paychecks.

However, you need to set up your file so that you enter these amounts manually, and the only way to tell QuickBooks that you want to exercise this option is through the Help menu.

1. Select QuickBooks Help from the main Help menu to open "Have a question"? Window or window.
2. In the Search box, enter Manual Payment Roll, and then click the Magnifying Glass icon (Search). QuickBooks features many helpful articles. Click on the article titled "Process

Payroll Manually (without a subscription to QuickBooks Payroll)."
3. Follow the instructions as described in "If you prefer to make manual payments." If you choose to process paid payers manually, you will still need to hire employees and pay rifles and pursue payment obligations.

The decision to operate a manual payment should only be made after careful consideration and consultation with your accountant, and if you have only one or two employees. It's up to you to make sure your calculations are accurate and that you have a handy system for making conversions at the right agency at the right time.

Prepare your salary

To produce accurate checks, you must add accounts to your checking account, create payroll items (salaries, wages, etc.); Specify the voltage taxes that you must withhold, payroll taxes that you must pay as an employer, company member or developer. You also need to provide tax information for all employees, such as dependents and absences.

You can either make these payment items either by using the Payroll Setup Wizard or manually. The following sections cover the steps to manually set the payment, and you will learn later how to use the Payroll

Setup Wizard. Check the two to determine how you want to do the setup.

Add payrolls to the card's accounts

You have to create new accounts in your account charts to get the level one. QuickBooks automatically adds salary and payroll calculations when you enable the payment. Use sub-accounts for payroll and payment expenses, as it makes it easy to track individual commitments and expenses. Make sure your payment transactions are linked to these accounts, not the original account. Then, when you generate reports, all balances in the parent accounts are collected.

Add vendors

Payment operation creates obligations for pay taxes and retained or deductible benefits from the salary. In QuickBooks, the government agency or employee has benefits

The amount you transfer must be a seller. Then, when you draw up a pay item that tracks retention or retention, you pass that item on to the appropriate provider.

To withhold federal income taxes, Medicare, the Federal Insurance Contributions Act (FICA), and Medicare and FICA-compliant employer payments, you can appoint the U.S. Treasury as a salesperson. As of January 1, 2011, the IRS has been requesting electronically with the EFTPS on all payroll taxes.

EFTPS deposits can be made online or over the phone, from the comfort of your home or office. If you have not already done so, you must visit the EFTPS website (www.eftps.gov) to learn more and register.

For local and state income taxes, unemployment, disability, employment, and severance benefits such as health insurance, create a vendor for any agency you need to pay. Most states now offer online payments for payment conversions on their websites, but if you use checks, you may have forms or coupons that must accompany your payments.

Add salary items

QuickBooks uses payment elements to list compensation or discount on a paycheck. Number of the individual payment elements that contain a check

Article description

Employee earnings can be those salaries. Hours, overtime, or double pay; In / or commissions.

Patients and / or vacation rates vary by industry and company policy.

Federal Taxes Federal Income Tax (FiT), Social Security (FICA), and Medicare.

Check the advanced income balance with your accountant on this item.

Local and local tax burdens These vary by state and local. Some regions have both state income and local income taxes.

State unemployment and disability These taxes vary by state, but almost every state has unemployment and disability taxes.

Pension or retirement plan These deductions vary by industry.

Insurance Medical deductions and life insurance.

These vary according to industry and local settings.

Decorations such as baby support, collection agencies, and the like.

Some Items on the List When enabling payroll services, typically include local taxes, medical benefits deductions, and other payment items. Existing items may also be missing sales information, so you'll need to change them accordingly.

To add a new payment item, select from the payment list window

| New or press CTRL-N to open the "New Payroll Item" window. Choose one of two ways to set up your payment points: EZ Setup or Custom Setup.

EZ preparation of payment elements

With the EZ Setup option, when you click Next, you will see a list of the types of payment points as described later. The descriptions are short, but you can create any kind of salary, discount or benefit, paid by the company, employee, or both. The only types of payment elements that you cannot create in the EZ preparation are government and local payroll taxes, including state unemployment and / or deficit taxes.

After selecting the item type, QuickBooks downloads the Payroll Setup Wizard and displays the Add New dialog box for this feature. The questions and explanations you see in the EZ Payroll Setup Wizard are more basic than the questions you ask when choosing the Adjustment option to set the payment item. You will need less knowledge about payment processing to complete the setup, but you will spend more time navigating between windows because most data you enter will find a window at the same time.

If you know nothing about payment suspension, benefits or accountability, and legal issues related to payment benefits and deductions, consult an accountant when it comes to payment. However, QuickBooks provides good explanations and is easy to understand for the required information.

For example, when drafting a provision such as health insurance, retirement, or interest in the cafeteria plan, QuickBooks asks whether the employee's company is fully loaded or fully shared or shared with both. Depending on your answer, you will go through the following window to set the required payment item (s).

In addition, if the employee contributes to some or all of the costs, you should find out if the pre-tax or decrease is after-tax, and you need to know how the payoff affects employees form W-2. This is another reason to discuss the first payment preparation with your accountant!

Custom setup for payroll

If you select the Custom Setup option, the list you see when you click "Next" is extensive. You can create all kinds of payment items displayed in the EZ Setup menu for Wage Types, and you can set up Government and Local Wage Items. You'll find it, differently

EZ Setup, every window in the Custom Setup Wizard, contains most fields to get the required information, which leads to fewer steps to complete Payroll Item Setup.

However, keep in mind that if you have a health benefit with shared costs between the company and the employee, the personalized setup wizard does not remind you that you should set up two elements: one deducts the number of the employee and another for the Pay company. In this case, you have to start the assistant again to select it

The company's contribution in the second assistant window to preparing the company from the side of the health benefits component.

Preparing staff

You have a lot of information to fill in for all employees, and some are probably the same for all or for most of your employees. The information about your employees must be accurate; otherwise, you will need to update payroll information within QuickBooks and then report changes to the IRS, both of which mean more work for you and potential confusion with the IRS about your payment data.

To save you a lot of time, you can create a new standard template for the employee. The information you place in the template is automatically added to the payroll tab for each new employee you create, as shown here.

Create an Employee Template

To access the template, open the Employee Center by selecting Employee / Center staff from the menu bar. In the Employee Center window, click the Manage Employee Information button at the top of the window and select "Change New Employee Default Settings" from the sub-menu that appears. This opens the Default Completed Employee Settings window, where you can enter data that is applicable to most or all of your employees.

1. Click on the column of the item name in the income box, and then click on the arrow to see a

list of the income types that you have selected as a payment item. Select the pattern that is frequent enough to match the template.
2. Enter in the hour / annual column. Enter the salary or salary number, if one applies to most of your employees. Otherwise, release it and enter every sentence in the employee record.
3. Click the arrow in the field to the right of the Payroll field and select a table.
4. Select a payment frequency (if you create tables and select one, QuickBooks automatically uses that table to fill the payment frequency field).
5. Use the class field when you enable classes to track data.
6. If you use QuickBooks, the time tracking features to pay for employee salaries, you will see the checkbox "Use time data to create checks". Select the checkbox to enable this feature.
7. If all or most of your employees have the same changes, click the Name column in the box Addition, Discount, and Company contributions, and then click the arrow to select the appropriate changes.
8. Click the Tax button to open the Tax Defaults dialog box, and select the common taxes that match the template. The status tab and the other tab (usually local pay taxes) contain tax data that is often applicable to all or most of your employees.

9. Click the "Sick / Vacation" button to set the conditions for collecting sick and vacation time, if your policy is similar enough among employees and to include the template.
10. When you are finished filling out the template, click OK to save it.

Create staff

You are ready to bring your employees. Staff Select Staff Center. Click on the New Employee button at the top of the window to add the first employee. The new employee form will be added to the Personal tab. Enter your new employee data, as shown here:

- Personal: Enter basic data about your new location.
- Address and Contact: Enter the address, phone number, email, and emergency contact information. You must have at least one W-2 file title.
- Additional Information: Use this tab to enter an employment number (optional) or create custom fields using the Select Fields button to track additional information.
- Payment Information: Enter profits, taxes, and discounts. (If you choose to enter a paycheck manually, this tab will be labeled "Compensation" and will not contain tax or bank transfer information.)

1. Click on the Tax button to open the Tax dialog box.
2. Enter federal and state tax information. QuickBooks builds and provides a lot of state information.
3. On the other tab, apply the local salary that applies to this employee.
4. Click on the sick / vacation button and enter the hours and dates of that employee.
5. When finished, click OK to return to the Payroll tab.

- Employment Information Enter your application date, employment details, and other work here. See "Understanding Recruitment Types" next to Selecting an Employee Type.

Understand the types of employment

There are four options in the Type field on the Employment Information tab of the new Employee Form. What you can indicate can have an impact on your tax returns, so check with your accountant if you have any questions. Table 4-4 shows the four varieties.

Statement type

The regular employee you hire and tax is exempt W-2.

If your job is not integrated, you have no officers. Employee Selection because the type has no effect on the operation of your paychecks (accounts, print checks, etc.); it only affects reports.

Legal The employee who works for you and who is regarded by the leave as an employee and not as an independent contractor. Check with your accountant before filing this type.

Employee payment tasks are not performed for this type of employee. This kind of employee is appropriate if you have a holding company because the landlord who pays you yourself is posted to an equity account called the retiree of the owner. If the company is a partnership, the amounts paid to the owner are distributed.

CHAPTER 7: PAY EMPLOYEES, PAY TAXES, AND CREATING FORMS

Handle Year Payment Data

To facilitate the introduction of historical data, consider using the payment service at the beginning of the calendar year. However, if you started using QuickBooks in the middle of the year, you should enter historical information about the payment checks that you have entered so far. In this way, QuickBooks can perform all the required end-of-year tasks. For example, you can't give your employees two W-2 forms: one from the Pre-QuickBooks system and the other from QuickBooks.

No matter what fiscal year you may be in, your payroll year is a calendar year. Even if you start using QuickBooks wages for the current period before you enter historical data, you should keep in mind that the lack of historical data will affect some taxes calculations. Also, year-to-year pay information on employee salaries will be incorrect until you enter historical pay data. If there are withheld quantities remaining after a certain amount, you will need to manually adjust the discounts on your current paycheck so that QuickBooks can calculate the maximum deduction correctly and cancel that amount.

Enter totals from year to date

If you are using the QuickBooks mid-year, you will need to enter your annual payday numbers so far in your QuickBooks file. Consider the following:

- You need to enter the total of all payment payments in the quarter, as 941 reports are generated every three months.
- You cannot enter summary data for the current quarter (the quarter in which the start date is). Instead, for the current quarter, you will need to enter data for each payment period (weekly, bi-annual, bi-monthly, or monthly). For previous chapters, you can enter quarterfinals.

Manually enter payroll and charges

Once you have introduced all of your employees, you can use a shortcut to begin the process of providing annual payroll information. This process copies old windows to the credit of using QuickBooks Payroll Setup, but some people find this method easier to use, especially if they choose to set their payments manually.

1. Select Help | About QuickBooks (2016 version) Desktop displays the product information

window. Then Press CTRL-SHIFT-Y. The YTD Amount Setup Wizard described later, walks you through the steps of entering the Annual Meeting of Annual Summaries. Click Next to start.
2. In the following two boxes, the assistant will ask you to specify three dates. It is important to note that the dates you enter are not the same as the three categories.

- • The date on which payroll and payroll accounts affect. When should you enter the data you enter for a user account and payment fees?
- • The date on which your bank accounts are considered. When should net paychecks be posted to your payday bank account?
- • The date of the first payment check verification that you create with QuickBooks Payroll. This salary will be published in all relevant accounts; there are no historical balances. When you enter this third date, click Next.

3. On the employee information page, you will see a list of employees. Highlight a name and click the Enter Summary button to open that employee's YTD adjustment window.
4. Provide YTD salary and booking allowance for each payment period. Click OK when you have completed the entries for each employee. You

return to the staff summary information page in the YTD Amount Setup Wizard. Click the Browse button to close the YTD Setup Wizard.

Choose the right dates when you pay from year to year

This example should help you understand how to enter the dates in these categories. For the purposes of these examples, let's say that you provide historical information.

At the end of April 2017, the first checks will be issued through QuickBooks on Friday, May 1, 2017.

- Your first submission of bonds and expenses will be April 1, 2017, because (hopefully) you have already transferred your rights and patronage contributions for the quarter ended March 31, 2017.
- The first release of your bank accounts must be May 1, 2017, the date of the first QuickBooks payment check.
- The date of "First Pay with QuickBooks" is the first payday in May. In this example, this day is May 1, 2017.
- Use the QuickBooks Menu Setup Wizard

When using the QuickBooks Menu Setup Wizard, to set your pay, the setup process may take longer than it takes to do these tasks manually. The wizard has several advantages: it's easy to use with full explanation, and you can use it to prepare all the necessary components for paying the salary, including entering your historical data. It also has a Finish Later button so you can open the place you interrupted when you reopen the wizard.

The QuickBooks Payroll Setup Wizard is divided into logical partitions.

Whether you are using the Payroll Setup Wizard to compile all your components or just enter historical data, be sure to set up all the providers and accounts you need to transfer your payment costs and patron costs to the employer.

Start by selecting Staff Set Payroll from the QuickBooks menu bar. The Wizard window opens with all the tasks listed in the left window. The first few screens are informative, indicating the data you will need to complete the assistant (the same information about employees, payroll elements, development, etc. The real work begins with the setup pages of the company, where the wizard begins to teach you the details needed to prepare your salary.

Company preparation department

In the "Company Setup" section, the assistant starts with compensation, which means payment elements, schedules, bonuses, etc. If you have already created your payment points, they will appear in the wizard window, and you can click Edit to view or change the settings. If you have not yet set up your payment items, click Add New to set up a small assistant to guide you through the process.

The types of remuneration assisted by the company manager department in the wizard include preparation of kinds of compensation, benefits, paid leave, supplements, and other deductions, such as worker companies, automatic expenses recovery, decorations, union fees, etc. In the.

Set up the staff and assistant

After the Company Setup section, the wizard goes into the Employee section. You can add all employees to the Wizard, and navigate through a series of windows where you enter personal information, pay structure, and tax status. For each employee, you can set taxes and benefits that affect the employee.

When you enter completed employee information, the assistant displays a list of employees. If any employee is missing information, the assistant will point out the problem. If you manually enter your employees, the assistant will automatically find your employee records and show you the same list if you have any problems.

Some missing information is not necessary for payroll payment, but QuickBooks requires information in the employee record. If any employee on the list has a "Fix it now" audit, that means that critical information is missing, and the system either cannot issue a check or fail to issue a W-2 form at the end of the year. Select the employee and click Edit to go through the wizard and fix the problem.

Set up payment taxes in the wizard

In the tax section, the therapist counts on the federal, state, and local taxes for which you are responsible. These are pay points, so if you don't have all these things set up in advance, you can use the wizard to do this now. After completion of each section, the assistant will display a list of all taxes for that section. If you manually set your taxes as additional items, the assistant will find these entries and use them to populate the list. If the assistant finds something wrong with your tax preparation, select Edit to make the desired changes.

Enter the salary record and the assistant

You can enter historical pay data in the Year by Date section. The wizard offers a panoply of windows, starting with a window asking if you have lunch checks this year besides QuickBooks. If you answered yes, the next window will be the Payroll Summary window, where you can access three pre-formatted tables. Click the Edit button next to each of these payment categories to open the associated worksheet and enter the information.

Run Data Review

Next is the data retention section, which is optional. QuickBooks asks if you want to override salary settings. If you select Yes, the wizard will run the payroll routine. At this point, your setup is complete, from here you can click Finish or go straight to the Payroll Center where you will have access to everything essential for Payroll Management.

Run the paycheck

You can pay the salary by making changes to the payment components (employees, taxes, etc.) by selecting employees Pay Service Run the Pay. The QuickBooks Payroll Setup Wizard takes you to a to-do list of payment items, and each section of the wizard's to-do list is scanned for errors. Scanning errors include missing information, invalid information, or other data that does not meet the payroll criteria included in QuickBooks.

- Pay

If your company pays employees and paid employees on a weekly basis and the worker pays every hour on a weekly basis, for example, using a paycheck makes it easy to ensure that you are paying for the right employees at the right time. When you create a payroll, you specify how often you pay your employees and specify the pay period (working days covered by salary), the date on the salary, and

Date of preparation of payment. (However, your salary preparation date is different from your payday if you are using direct deposit, and require that you transfer your payment information two days before the payday.)

Manage your salary

You can also create payrolls at other times. When employees choose salaries, in addition to the planned salary sub-salary, you see two things for having a special salary:

- Unscheduled Payroll Select this special payment category if you need to create additional checks, commission checks, or any other payment type that differs from the regularly selected payment.
- Final Examination - To use this option, you must first enter a release date on the Employment Information tab in the Employee Record. Make sure this release date is after the verification date because QuickBooks runs the name from the payroll information window from that date, which means you can't create a final paycheck for that person.

When you're ready to create the verification, select the terminated employee by checking the column at the top of the employee's name. Then fill in the payment period.

Expiration Date, Check Date, Expiration Date, and Hours (or Amount Calculated by Employee). Click Continue to accept or change salary details, then print the check, set the check number for a manual check, or issue a direct deposit check.

- Payment is running

When you are ready to run your first payment, a payment check will begin as follows:

- If you are not using payroll, select Employees | Pay Employee Unscheduled Payment Opens the Enter Pay Pie Information dialog box.
- If you have pay, select Employees | Paying Employee Scheduled Payroll to open the Staff Center with the selected Payments tab (the "Employee Payment" feature appears in the right shade). Select the appropriate schedule and click Start Payment to open the Payment Information dialog box.

Choose employees to pay. If all employees receive paychecks (the usual scenario), click Verify All. For hourly staff configured to receive automatic payments by airplane, the number of hours is pre-populated. For employees whose wages are not paid per hour schedule, you will need to fill in the number of hours for that salary.

Salary change

If you want to make changes to a paycheck, click Employee Name to open the Pay Preview dialog box. You can add a salary element like a bonus, submit a paycheck to a client or a job, or add a discount like a loan repayment or decoration. Click Save & Next to go to the next employee, click Save & Previous to return to a previous review, or click "Save & Close" to return to the Enter Payroll Information dialog box. If you want to make a change to a paycheck after you print it, you will need to "open" the information to make that change. Contact your payment specialist before doing this for the first time.

Check the salary

Click on "Continue" in the "Enter Payroll Information" dialog box to display the "Review and Create Payroll" window that triggers all the financial information for this payment. If anything seems to be wrong, click Back to reconfigure the checks or make any other necessary corrections.

Fill out the options to produce the check checks (print checks or add check numbers automatically to your bank account for manual checks), and then click Create Check Checks. QuickBooks creates tests and displays the confirmation dialog in the following steps.

If you print paychecks, you can print to paychecks, or you can wait and print them by clicking File | Printing Forms Print out the pie as described later. If you have employees who make direct deposits, click Print Pay Stubs. When payment support is printed, click on the "send payment details" button in the confirmation and next steps dialog box. This opens the Send Center window, and you can directly upload depot data and intuition for processing. You can send payment items by email using the included security standards (see help files for details).

If you have a different payment plan to run today (you can be paid every two weeks and employees every two weeks today), repeat all operations as shown here.

The information of your employees is stored in the personnel center.

- Staff center

All the employee information you enter and the payroll and paychecks you create are easily accessible through the Staff Center. The Staff Center contains payment reporting information and provides links to all payment functions. It is a central place for everything you have to do or need to know.

QUICKBOOKS

To open this window, select Employees | Center staff from the menu bar. When you subscribe to the QuickBooks Payroll service, the real damage to the Staff Center includes three tabs: Employees, Transactions, and Payroll. If you do not have a payment plan subscription, the section lacks a payroll tab.

Employees Tab

When you select an employee on the Employee tab, QuickBooks displays employee record information at the top left and transaction information for that employee at the bottom of the left pane. You can change the options in the Show fields and Date fields to filter transaction information. Note the three additional tabs that are directly above the employee transaction information. It allows you to add and manage tasks, notes, and emails to the employee.

You can open any listed transaction by double-clicking it. For example, if you open a check, you can see the original check with a summary of the financial information. If you need to review details, click on Paycheck Detail to see all calculated amounts.

Transaction Tab

The transaction tab lists all types of payment agreements. Select a type to see the transactions you created. You can use the date field to shorten the offer of information.

144

Pay

On the Payroll tab, you can view future liability payments (and those that may be required), create transactions, and create the payment forms you need. Visit this tab regularly to make sure you don't miss a deadline.

Allocation of staff center

You can update the Staff Center view of the information. Change the pan by moving the cursor over the edge of any part; when the pointer changes to a vertical bar with the left and right arrows, push the part in either direction. In addition, you can expand the pan to display the entire list view by clicking the arrow button at the top of the Employees tab. Use the same button to collapse the field to display both the menu and the details pane.

You can customize the columns that QuickBooks displays in the left-hand section of the Employees tab by right-clicking anywhere in the list and customizing.

Sailing. You can also personalize the information in the right pane if you choose an employee name on the employee tab or if you select a transaction type on the transaction tab. Right-click anywhere in the left (Transactions) pane and select Customize Columns.

- Pursue payment obligations accordingly

All the tasks involved in reporting and paying income obligations with QuickBooks have a logical order, although the steps may vary depending on the state and municipality in which you are located.

Confirm payment switch

If you have a payment role, QuickBooks keeps a payment schedule behind the scenes that tracks the sums and amounts of all payment and employer obligations.

Expenses that accumulate: Use this payment plan to ensure that payroll obligations are transferred on time. Most of the required information for scheduling payments may already be in your system when you set up paychecks. To view the table and correct any issues, select Employees | Taxes on salaries and liabilities Change payment date/forms of payment.

This opens the Payroll Wizard tax payment window. While navigating through each page, if the data is missing or does not fit the content or format that the payment system expects, the wizard displays the list with the problem code. Double-click on the list of topics to edit and resolve. QuickBooks usually provides an indication of the problem in the window that opens.

Report and Transfer Income Tax Bonds

When you create payment checks, QuickBooks tracks taxes, which are considered a liability. To see your planned commitments, select Employees | Taxes on salaries and liabilities Payment of planned commitments. The Pay tab shows a list of other taxes and connections currently in place,

Select the liability you want to pay and click on the View / Pay button. The first time you pay obligations, QuickBooks asks you to choose the appropriate bank account (if you have more than one). The Payment window opens. Continue to offer and pay until all current payment obligations are set.

Federal tax bonds

Payments to the federal government involve payment taxes:

- 941/944/943 Taxes, Withholding, Social Security, and Medical Care
- 940 taxes are the federal unemployment taxes

941/943 Payments The Federal Government requires that you report and transfer eligible funds, along with identical employer contributions, at a specified time. This time period depends on the total amount you have collected. You may be asked to transfer the month, half month, weekly, or within three days of your payment. Check the current limits with your IRS or accountant.

There is a formula to determine the size of the charge 941/943. This is the sum of these sums for the period: Federal Withholding, plus FICA (Social Security)

Source changes, in addition to Medicare Medication, as well as identical employer contributions to FICA and Medicare.

You don't have to do math - QuickBooks does it for you. But it is a good idea to know the formula you are using so you can verify the numbers yourself and make sure you have enough funds in your bank account to cover your next payment.

In addition, the IRS requires you to transfer your payments electronically, either through the QuickBooks enhanced payment or through the IRS Electronic Tax Payment System (EFTPS); the beneficiary is the U.S. Treasury. If you have not already done so, you must visit the EFTPS website (www.eftps.gov) to learn

More in registration. However, if your employment tax for a quarter is less than $2,500, you can transfer the tax with a quarterly return (Form 941) instead of deducting it.

Create Form 941/943 Unless you are a Form 944 blogger (where the annual payout amount is less than $ 1,000 per year), you must submit Form 941 or 943 every three months to report the total amount you report to the Federal Government Income Tax and FICA A

Medicare. If you cancel your deposits regularly and on time, there will be no amount with 941/943.

- If you receive low salaries, you can use the EFTPS system to transfer your payments for a low payment amount or transfer payment with your form using a check paid to the U.S. Treasury.
- If you have paid over, you can choose the option to get a balance against the next 941/943, or you can choose a repayment option.

QuickBooks prepares your 941/943 report by using the information in your payment record in QuickBooks. If QuickBooks does not create federal forms (either because you make payments manually or you are signed up for QuickBooks Basic Payroll), you can create forms manually using Excel worksheets

Delivered by QuickBooks. See the "Tax Form Worksheets in Excel" section at the end of this chapter. Creating a form is very easy.

1. Selection of Personnel | Paid Tax Forms and W-2s | Practical payment forms. The Payroll tab opens in the Employee Center to see a list of tax forms available for deposit.
2. Select Federal Quarter Form 941 / Sch B - Patron Quarter Tax Statements (or Federal Quarter Form 943A - Annual Patron Quarterly

for Farmers) and click on the Form Quarter button. The file form file opens.
3. Select the deposit period. You can also click the AutoFill Contact Info button to automatically copy QuickBooks the contact information you provide in this window to future tax forms that you must make. Click OK.
4. The Window Tax Form window opens on the selected form. The first window is an interview. Enter the appropriate data and click Next to continue.
5. Use the instructions in the following sections to navigate through the wizard.

To enter the information into an empty field, click on the cursor in the field to activate it, and then enter the data. Text appears in blue, but this is just a tip to you that the data has been entered manually; QuickBooks does not print the form in color.

Changing pre-filled data

Follow these steps to edit the data:

1. Right-click on the field and select Overlays from the menu that appears.
2. Enter the alternate data in the bypass box and press the TAB key.
3. The new data replaces the original data in the field, and the text is green to remind you that

you have exported the data manually from QuickBooks.

If you change your mind and decide that the data that QuickBooks automatically delivers should remain on the form, right-click in the field and select "Overwrite."

Data you cannot change

Do not change the following types of data in Form 941 or in a payroll tax form:

- Federal Patent Identification Number (EIN)
- Submission period (if you try to change the submission period, restart the process and select the appropriate date range)
- Total (calculated from QuickBooks; if the sum is incorrect, the wrong number changes, QuickBooks calculates the sum again)

Check for faults

Before completing the Form 941/943 content, click on the Check Error button. QuickBooks scans the content and displays any errors in the error box that occur at the top of the form. If there are no problems, the error box will also report this.

Click on any error to automatically move to the field that is causing the problem, and then correct the information:

- If the problem is in a field that you have filled in, correct the data, and press the TAB key.
- If the problem is in a predefined field, but you have changed the content by overwriting the data, right-click with a field, and select "Override."

If you press TAB to replace the data in the field, the error list should disappear from the error box. If not, you should find out and correct the data errors. If you correct the error, you can close the error box by clicking the Error button.

Save to an incomplete form again

If you are cutting while preparing Form 941, 943, or 940, you can save it with the data you have already filled out so that you do not have to start cutting when you go back. Click Save and Close to save the form with its current content. To go back to the saved form, you must re-open the form, following the steps from the previous section, and select the shape and date range again. QuickBooks asks if you want to use the saved draft. When making changes, you must start a new template instead of opening a saved draft. Changes may include an additional check issued during the date range for any reason, or payments made to the IRS, as a transfer during this reporting period.

Print or submit Form 941/943

You can print the form from QuickBooks, save it as a PDF, or send the form electronically. When deciding to print, be sure to use these printing criteria:

- The form should be printed in black ink on white paper or cream paint.
- The paper size should be 8.5 by 11 inches.
- The weight of the paper should be 20 pounds or heavier.

The printed report does not resemble the one-sided model you received, but it is fully accepted by the government. Print two copies: one for emailing and one for your files.

The Federal Unemployment Tax Act (FUTA) provides unemployment compensation to workers who have lost their jobs, usually after the state benefits of workers have been exhausted. FUTA tax is paid by employers; no rejection of the salary of the employees. Companies must make FUTA payments if none of the following scenarios exist:

- This year or last year, I paid at least $1500 in each calendar quarter.
- At least this year or last year, you had at least part of the day for 20 weeks one or more employees (weeks should not be closed).

You do not have to make the deposit until you owe the full amount, but you can make deposits until you reach that amount if you want.

Currently, the FUTA tax is 6 percent of the total salary of $7,000 per employee, but the federal government is giving employers up to 5.4 percent of credit for paying unemployment taxes in the state. So, if you qualify for a maximum balance of 5.4 percent, the FUTA tax rate after the balance is 0.6 percent. QuickBooks assumes that you pay your state taxes and calculate your FUTA obligations accordingly.

Form 940 (FUTA) is presented annually. To build the 940 shapes:

1. Selection of Personnel | Paid Tax Forms and W-2s | Practical payment forms. The Payroll tab opens in the Employee Center to see a list of tax forms available for deposit.
2. Determine the Annual Form 940 / Sch A - FUTA for the employer. Click the File Form button to open the File Form window.
3. Select the deposit period. You can also click the AutoFill Contact Info button to automatically copy QuickBooks the contact information you provide in this window to future tax forms that you must make. Click OK.
4. The Income Tax Form Window (the first window of the Assistant) is displayed with a 940 interview. Under this section, a series of

questions is designed to determine if any of your payment costs covers covered payment types. Payments made are the wages you paid that are exempt from FUTA taxes. QuickBooks checks your payment points to track different categories of exempt payments, and if you used these payment items, QuickBooks completes the quantities. If you have any free payments that are not in the payment items that QuickBooks automatically checks, fill in the amount immediately in the appropriate field. Check the IRS rules for preparing Form 940, or check with your accountant. You can also get more information about this form by clicking on the "Details about this form" link at the bottom of the Payroll Tax Form window.

5. Click Next to see the form itself. Fill in fields that are not automatically included by QuickBooks in your payment items. Continue clicking Next and follow the on-screen instructions.

State and local income tax

Your local and state salary obligations will vary depending on your business and where you live (and pay taxes). In addition to income taxes, you can be responsible for unemployment and disability insurance. Most states have some form of income tax that can be calculated as a fixed or slippery percentage of total income or as a percentage based on an federal tax on an employee.

Local taxes (municipal or local) vary far from the approach:

- Different cities have different rates for employees of businesses operating in the city. It can be a rate for employees living in the same city, and another rate for non-residents.
- Your business can operate in a city or city where taxpayers are paid (one-time pay per year, a fixed amount per employee).

QuickBooks Enhanced Payroll supports most case models. State and local tax authorities offer vouchers, forms, or online income tax services. The frequency you have to pay may depend on the size of your salary, or it may be quarterly, semi-annually, or yearly, regardless of the amount. Some municipal authorities have available online payment.

It is advisable to create different unemployment insurance (SUI) names, Government Disability Insurance (SDI) names and withhold the state income tax to ensure that the checks are not sent in error to the wrong component and to prevent

QuickBooks publish a check for the total. The sales record for each sales name may have the same beneficiary (FCO), but the sales names are different.

Other state bonds

If your state has SUI, SDI, or both, you will have to pay those bonds if they fail. Usually, these are quarterly payments. Not all countries have SUI or SDI, and some have one and not the other. Some countries collect SUI and SDI from employees and company; others collect only by the company. Please check the rules of your state or speak to an accountant.

Non-tax Payroll

The rules for transmitting salary reductions and employer contributions for other reasons, such as health benefits, pensions, and workers' compensation, are specific to your arrangements with these providers. There are many ways to take care of how these payments are released, and you have to decide what makes sense in your account. For example, if you make a monthly payment to a medical insurance company, you may want to get your employee reductions back to the same expense account you use to pay your bill. Thus, the net amount is only recorded as the cost of your taxes.

To convert commitments that are not a scheduled bond into QuickBooks, you can use the Unscheduled Commitments window. Staff Select Taxes on Salaries and Liabilities Make personalized liability payments. Select the target date range you need, and then select the responsibility you want to transfer.

QUICKBOOKS

Labor camp

Expanded QuickBooks and Pay Offers contain worker companies, and setup options are in the "Payroll" and "Employees" categories in the "Preferences" dialog box. Click the Workers Compensation button on the Company Preferences tab to open the Work Preferences dialog. Select Track Workers Comp to enable this feature.

When Workers Comp is enabled, you can also choose to see reminders to set worker company codes when creating checks or schedules. Additionally, you can choose the option to exclude overtime premiums from your workers' accounts (see your worker's insurance policy to see if you can calculate overtime as a normal wage).

- Preparation of W-2 models

On or before January 31 of each year, you must print and send W-2 forms to your employees for the previous year. By February 28, you must also send or copy electronic files to the appropriate government agencies. Running your Payroll and QuickBooks makes this process easy. You begin by selecting the form and employee and then go through the process of creating, printing, or submitting forms electronically. Let's do it:

1. Selection of Personnel | Paid Tax Forms and W-2s | Practical payment forms. The Payroll tab

opens in the Employee Center to see a list of tax forms available for deposit.
2. Select the Annual Form W-2 / W-3 - Payment Statement and Tax / Transfer. Click on the sample file button. The File Form dialog box opens.
3. Select the application period and the staff you want to process the W-2 forms. You can also click the AutoFill Contact Info button to automatically copy QuickBooks the contact information you provide in this window to future tax forms that you must make. Click OK.
4. The "Selection of employees for Form W-2 / W-3" window appears, showing all your employees who received a check during the year, as shown here. By default, all employees are selected, and the current state of the W-2 printing process is observed.
5. Click "Review / Change" to display the first page of the Payroll Tax Form window, which explains the steps to follow when navigating through the wizard. Click Next to go through the wizard.
6. In the following screens, a W-2 form is presented to each employee. If any non-financial data is missing (such as address or zip code), you will need to fill it out. If the pre-filled information is incorrect, right-click on the appropriate field and select override. Enter the correct information and press TAB to add this

they can view and print their W-2 information directly from the Intuit website called ViewMyPaycheck.com. Also, when employees use TurboTax to prepare their personal tax returns, they can view and download W-2 forms directly into TurboTax. To learn more about this service, click the Tell Me More link in the Print W-2 and W-3 Forms window.

- Tax Form Worksheets in Excel

If QuickBooks does not set up your payment forms (either because you make payments manually or you are registered for the QuickBooks Basic Payroll service), you can manually submit the forms using Excel worksheets available from QuickBooks.

To access the Worksheets, select Reports | Employees, and Salaries More Payment Reports in Excel | Tax form works as shown here. Because the Excel file contains macros, depending on how you configure the Excel security options, you must tell Excel to run the macros.

When the QuickBooks Tax Worksheets dialog box appears, select the form and registration period you need. Next, click on the "Options / Settings" button to open the Quick Box Options / Options / Settings options dialog box in QuickBooks, where you create the report.

By default, the Worksheet Header option is selected. This means that the printed header of the worksheet contains the company name and address information, as well as the report data area (the date range you selected in the previous dialog box). If you want to print the report, you need to know the date range, then be sure to select this option. By default, the Hide detailed data hidden from the QuickBooks option is selected, which means that the workbook only displays information with the report you selected.

When you clear the Hide Detail Data option, QuickBooks adds a second worksheet called Data to the workbook. This worksheet contains detailed information about employees, pay elements, and labor cost links (when using timelines to make significant pay) and individual rows.

Microsoft Office 2010, 2013, and 2016 products are available in both 32-bit and 64-bit editions. If you are using a 64-bit version of Excel, look for alternative power

The available connection method for the Excel 64-bit option (located in QuickBooks Tax Forms Workbooks - Options / Settings dialog box) to complete the export process.

- Use QuickBooks electronic file

If you choose to subscribe to QuickBooks Enhanced Payroll, you can submit forms 941, 940, W-2, and W-3 using the QuickBooks electronic file. Let's do it:

1. Change the way you save the form you want to send to the e-file by selecting Employee/Pay Center.
2. Click Install QuickBooks | Tax Form Related Activities Changing Payment Date / Payment Forms Schedule of Payments.
3. Click the form you want to send to the electronic file and select Edit. Turns the payment method into an electronic file.

After making your changes to QuickBooks, within about 10 to 14 days, you will receive a 10-digit PIN to use when uploading these forms.

If the form is, submit the form to QuickBooks.

1. Click Payment Form Processing.
2. Check out the form below.
3. Click on Submit Mail File Form.
4. Enter your contact information and the 10-digit PIN you receive.

Made in the USA
Coppell, TX
14 December 2019

information to the field. Changes you make to non-financial information will not be returned to the Employee Register. You should make the same changes there.

7. Click on the "Check Error" button to see if something is wrong in the form of an employee. If errors appear in the error box at the top of the form, click on the error list. QuickBooks automatically brings you to the appropriate field to correct the information.

8. If everything is correct, load the W-2 forms into the printer (even if you are electronic, you are likely to print the copy that goes to the employee) and click on "Send Form" for the dialog " Print / Mail "Open Dialog Form In.

9. If you enroll in the Agency's electronic filing program, have an active income plan, and there are no errors in the form, the option to email these forms is sent to you. Otherwise, only the Print button is active. Select the option to open the W-2 and W-3 Shapes window.

10. Click "Print" if all these settings are the way you want. You should also print or print the W-3 electronic form, which is a summary of your W-2 forms.

You can make your employees' W-2 forms available online at no extra cost if you have a QuickBooks payment plan. Use of this service eliminates the need to print and mail W-2 forms to your employees, where